Experimenting With & Within Architecture Competitions

The Competition Grid

RIBA Publishing

© RIBA Publishing, 2018

Published by RIBA Publishing, 66 Portland Place, London, W1B 1NT

ISBN 978-1-85946-710-7 / 978-1-85946-737-4 (PDF)

British Library Cataloguing-in-Publication Data

A catalogue record for this book is available from the British Library.

Commissioning Editor: Alexander White

Project Editor: Daniel Culver

Production: Richard Blackburn

Designed and typeset by Kalina Norton/Studio Kalinka

Printed and bound by Page Bros, Norwich, UK

Cover image/Image credits: www.shutterstock.com

www.ribapublishing.com

ACKNOWLEDGEMENTS

This publication was made possible thanks to the generous contribution of a large group of acclaimed scholars and practitioners, who kindly responded to the editors' call, by offering original material, and remaining available throughout the book's assemblage. All contributors have heartily engaged with the editors in the long process of development that such a project entails.

We gratefully acknowledge the generous sponsorship from Leeds Beckett University which allowed for the images in the book to be coloured. We are especially indebted to the Dean of the School of Art, Architecture and Design, Dr Lisa Stansbie; she not only supported this publication full-heartily, but she also actively backed the 6th International Competition Conference on Architectural Competitions (ICC 2016), organised at Leeds Beckett in 2016. Although the idea for the book has preceded the conference, the latter provided additional grounds for discussion and exchange of ideas, as well as new and exciting concepts to explore in the elaboration of the book's contents, thus decidedly taking the project a step further.

Special thanks go to Magnus Rönn and his team of fellow scholars, for their ever-lasting fascination with the subject of competitions, perseverance and scientific rigor. They have offered both inspiration and practical guidance for the production of this book, as well as for the ICC 2016 conference, and for this the editors remain grateful.

Finally, we would like to thank RIBA's external reviewers for their constructive comments and the editorial team of RIBA Publishing, especially Alex White and his predecessor Fay Gibbons; their professional skills have greatly contributed in bringing this project smoothly to its successful completion.

CONTENTS

Dr Maria Theodorou, PhD (AA), architect ARB/RIBA, Fulbright visiting fellow (Princeton 2005). Maria has been the director and founding member of the independent *School of Architecture for All* (SARCHA) and a senior lecturer at Leeds School of Architecture. A juror and organizer of international architecture competitions, she was recently invited expert for the selection of the 2018 Venice Biennale Belgian pavilion. Her research, publications and teaching centers on 'architecture and the political' and has lectured internationally and published widely. She is co-organiser of the *Shadow Series* (2016-17) and the *Ricochet Series* (2017-18) at the Architectural Association in London.

Antigoni Katsakou, PhD (EPFL), M Arch (UPC), Dipl Arch (NTUA) is a London-based architect (ARB) and author. She has been Visiting Fellow at the Bartlett School of Graduate Studies (2012-13) and has lectured in the United Kingdom, Switzerland and Greece, presented her work worldwide and been awarded with research and travel grants. She has published on architectural competitions in several languages, including the co-authored *Concevoir des logements. Concours en Suisse 2000-2005 [Designing Apartments; Competitions in Switzerland 2000-2005]*. Her interest in competitions stems from residential architecture and design innovation; she has also worked on housing cooperatives and urban regeneration, architectural representation and its social meaning, the perceptual experience of space and visual effects of layout geometries.

CONTRIBUTORS' BIOGRAPHIES

ESSAYS' CONTRIBUTORS

Marina Bos-de Vos MSc, PhD Candidate at the Department of Management in the Built Environment, Delft University of Technology. Marina performs her research in the context of futurA, a four-year research project on governance and business models for architectural services funded by the Dutch Science Foundation (www.future-architect.nl). In her work, Marina particularly focuses on value creation and value capture by architectural firms and the specific tensions that these firms encounter in their business models. Building on management literature, empirical data collection in architectural firms and client organisations and her background as a practicing architect, Marina translates theoretical insights into strategic decision-making frameworks to support architects in arriving at sustainable business strategies.

Robert Hammond, Co-Founder and Executive Director Friends of the High Line. Robert Hammond is the Co-Founder and Executive Director of Friends of the High Line, a nonprofit conservancy that he co-founded with Joshua David in 1999. Hammond has been awarded the Vincent Scully Prize (2013), the Rome Prize by the American Academy in Rome (2010), the Rockefeller Foundation's Jane Jacobs Medal, along with David (2010), and an honorary doctorate from The New School (2012). Hammond is a graduate of Princeton University; he is also a self-taught artist and served as an ex-officio member of the Metropolitan Museum of Art's Board of Trustees. Hammond is a co-producer of the film *Citizen Jane: Battle for the City*, released via IFC in April 2017.

Kristian Kreiner is Professor Emeritus at Copenhagen Business School, Department of Organization. In his organizational studies, he has covered a long list of themes and subjects, including decision making, sense making, project management, and culture. For many years, his empirical field of research has been the building industry. He has published repeatedly on architectural competitions, having done ethnographic studies of competition design, architects' production of design proposals, and the decision processes of juries.

Florian Kossak is Senior Lecturer for Urban History, Theory and Design at the Sheffield School of Architecture where he is founding member of AGENCY. He studied architecture in Berlin and Glasgow and received his PhD from the Edinburgh College of Art. He was co-founder of the co-operative GLAS ltd. He has curated exhibitions in Germany, France, Italy and the UK and is author of numerous articles, architectural monographs, and catalogues concerned with the mediation of architecture and urbanism.

Hélène Lipstadt received her doctorate from the École des Hautes Études en Sciences Sociales, Paris, after studying anthropology at the London School of Economics. She has published studies of competitions since their resurrection in France in the 1980s, most prominently in her essays in *The Experimental Tradition* (1989). Her current focus is on the conception of the competitions as an instantiation of the field of cultural production within the field of power, as theorized by Pierre Bourdieu. She has argued for its broader use, offering as examples of its utility analyses of the competitions for the memorial to Thomas Jefferson colloquially known as the St. Louis Arch, the Berlin Jewish Museum, and in preparation, The League of Nations (1927).

Walter Menteth RIBA, FRIAS is an architect, planner, writer and educationalist. He is a director of Walter Menteth Architects, Project Compass CIC, a procurement intelligence and competitions service, is a founder member of thefulcrum.eu, a digital pan-European architectural competitions and procurement intelligence network and part time lecturer at the Portsmouth School of Architecture. Walter is an RIBA National Councilor 2011-2017, was chair of the RIBA Procurement Reform Group 2011-2013 and synthesised many of the RIBA's responses during consultations stages leading to adoption of Public Works Directive EU 2014/24. He was a member of the UK Cabinet Office SME Panel 2011-2015. Walter has been recipient of: the RIBA President's Medal for Research, RIBA President's Award for Practice-located Research, and a number of national building design awards. He has won and judged various architectural competitions, and written extensively on competitions and procurement.

Tiina Merikoski is a landscape architect M.Sc. and a PhD candidate at the Aalto University Department of Build Environment. Her main interests of research have been sustainable land use, transformative innovations, transdisciplinary knowledge production, and the image as a design tool. In her research, she has been working with architectural competition projects as well as with the development of tourism destinations. Currently she explores these themes also as a consultant. Her research has been funded by Aalto University, the Finnish Cultural Foundation, and the Jenny and Antti Wihuri Foundation.

Aymone Nicolas was born in Mostaganem and grew up in black Africa. From 1990 to 1995 she studied at the École supérieure des Beaux-Arts and the Faculty of Letters in Montpellier. Then she went on to study history of the 20th century architecture at the University Panthéon-Sorbonne, where she completed her Doctorate degree in 2002 under the guidance of Prof. Gérard Monnier. Her PhD on UIA and architecture and urban design competitions between 1948 and 1975 was published by Editions Picard in 2007. She then taught at the School of Architecture of Paris-Malaquais and worked as a scholar at the German Centre of Art History in Paris (DFGK) from 2000 to 2006. Having spent several years in Berlin, during her studies, she organised various study trips for French architects in the German capital, and also in Vorarlberg and Hambourg. Since 2007, she lives in the south of France and works as a tutor in the field of ecological construction, at the cooperative society Ecoterre.

Magnus Rönn, Associate Professor, The School of Architecture, Royal Institute of Technology, Stockholm, Sweden. Magnus had a position as research leader at the School of Architecture to 2017. In 2006 he was qualified as Professor in architecture by Professor Anne Marie Wilhelmsen. Together with colleagues Magnus has been editor in chief for publishing four special issues on competitions in scientific journals, The *Nordic Journal of Architectural Research* (2009, No 2/3; 2012, No 1) and *FROMakademisk* (2013, No 4; 2014, No 1). He has published five books on competitions, two anthologies in English (2008, 2013, 2016) and two monographs in Swedish (2005, 2013).

Birgitte Sauge is senior curator in the Architecture Department at the National Museum of Art, Architecture and Design and editor of the Norwegian scientific journal *Norsk museumstidsskrift*. She has a doctorate in art history from the University of Bergen (2004). Her research focuses on architectural competitions, exhibitions and architectural representations. 2016-2019 she holds a research position in the interdisciplinary project Architecture Museums and Digital Design Media, part of the larger project *Mediascapes – Cultural Heritage Mediascape*, organized by the Department of Education, University of Oslo and financed by the Norwegian Research Council.

Judith Strong was employed initially by the Royal Institute of British Architects to develop, promote and manage the Competition System before joining The Arts Council of Great Britain to administer the government's capital funding programme for the arts. She subsequently set up the consultancy 'Arts and Architecture Projects', specialising in guiding and supporting clients through the initial stages of building projects. Her publications include *Participating in Architectural Competitions*; *Winning by Design*; *The Arts Council Guide to Building for the Arts*; *Theatre Buildings – A Design Guide*; and case studies of lottery funded and competition winning buildings.

Jeremy Till is an architect, educator and writer. He is Head of Central Saint Martins and Pro Vice-Chancellor for Research at the University of the Arts London. Till's extensive written work includes the books *Flexible Housing*, *Architecture Depends* and *Spatial Agency,* all three of which won the prestigious RIBA President's Award for Research. As an architect, he worked with Sarah Wigglesworth Architects on their pioneering building, 9 Stock Orchard Street, winner of many awards including the RIBA Sustainability Prize. He curated the UK Pavilion at the 2006 Venice Architecture Biennale and also at the 2013 Shenzhen Biennale of Architecture and Urbanism.

Elisabeth Tostrup is Professor Emerita at the Oslo School of Architecture and Design. She was a practising architect and won prizes in important competitions in Norway, and in 1993 first prize in the EAAE essay competition. Tostrup received her Ph.D. in

1996 on the thesis which is the basis for the book *Architecture and Rhetoric: Text and Design in Architectural Competitions*, London, 1999. She has published widely on Scandinavian 20th century architecture, among which *Norwegian Wood. The thoughtful architecture of Wenche Selmer*, New York, 2006 and *Planetveien 12. The Korsmo House. A Scandinavian Icon*, London 2014.

Dr. Leentje Volker, Associate Professor of Public Commissioning at Delft University of Technology. Focusing on architecture and infrastructure from a public client perspective, Leentje studies the interaction between people and the built environment on the individual, organizational and institutional level. Key topics in her work include organisational decision making, project governance and design competitions. In her research, she combines a psychological perspective on design with management sciences to gain innovative insights on the origin of (potential) conflicts in decision processes within the public realm. The combination of her scientific and managerial activities inspires her to work towards practical solutions of complex issues with a scientific underpinning.

DISCUSSIONS' CONTRIBUTORS

Philip D. Allsopp, D.Arch, RIBA, FRSA, CSBA President, RIBA USA Americas Region, Senior Sustainability Scientist, Arizona State University, Global Institute of Sustainability, Chief Design Officer, Smart Pad Living, LLC (www.smartpadliving.com). Phil is a Chartered Architect and holds a master's degree in health services planning and design from Columbia University, New York. Following U.S. Government service as a Public Health Service Fellow in Washington, D.C., Phil held practice leadership positions with global firms in the fields of architecture (Perkins and Will) and, for the bulk of his career, in health care management consulting and system dynamics (EDS, A.T. Kearney and Blue Shield of California). Phil was President and CEO of the Frank Lloyd Wright Foundation through 2010 and is a Senior Sustainability Scientist at Arizona State University's Global Institute of Sustainability.

Tom Bloxham MBE is chairman and founder of award-winning regeneration company Urban Splash, which has received nearly 400 awards to date for architecture, design and business success. The company is responsible for development projects across the country, including Manchester, Liverpool, Birmingham, Leeds, Bradford, Sheffield, Bristol, Plymouth and Morecambe. In 1999 Tom was awarded an MBE for Services to Architecture and Urban Regeneration. Tom also upholds a number of other positions including; Chairman of Manchester International Festival, and trustee of Tate, the Manchester United Foundation and The Bloxham Charitable Trust.

Angel Borrego Cubero (Spain, 1967) is trained in architecture, with a PhD from ETSA Madrid and a MArch from Princeton University, where he was a Fulbright scholar. He has been teaching and practising architecture since the '90s while also developing an interdisciplinary body of works dealing with issues such as the contemporary urban condition, the negotiations between private and public space, violence, surveillance and fictions in architecture. He won Best Adaptive Reuse at NAN Awards'16, First Prize COAM '14 (Architects Association of Madrid), a Dissemination Award and a Research Award at the XIII Spanish

Architecture Biennial. He was part of the Golden Lion awarded Spanish Pavilion at the XV Biennale di Venezia.

Angela Brady OBE PDSA PPRIBA FRIAI, graduated from DIT, then won a scholarship to Copenhagen and worked in Toronto. Set up award winning Brady Mallalieu Architects with Robin Mallalieu in 1987 in London, specialising in contemporary sustainable architecture & urban design. Given 100 keynote speeches around the world on sustainable city making. Chairs Croydon Place Review Panel, VC of Bexley Review Panel, and Design Council 'Built Environment Expert'. Angela co wrote/presented with Dr Sandra O'Connell TV series *Designing Ireland* broadcast on RTE. Past president of RIBA. Received OBE 2016 & PDSA 2017 (President's Distinguished Service Award) from Michael D Higgins, both for services to architecture.

Tim Clark DipArch (London), MA (York), FRAS, RIBA, M.ASCE, Hon. FICWCI Currently with Deutsche Bahn responsible for architectural input to heavy engineering and master-planning on GCC long distance Railway and Doha Metro (2010-). Regional Director with

ATKINS UK (2007-10) seconded as Director of Architecture, Dubai Metro (2008-9). Principal, CLARK+KANNER (Los Angeles 1995-2007), First Chapter Chair RIBA Los Angeles (1995-2004); RIBA Country Representative (1996). Founding President RIBA-USA (1996-2005), now President Emeritus. Architect of Oil-related, off-grid rainforest and orphanage projects in Cameroon; Aga Khan Prize nominee (1998); Honorary Professor at the University of Yaoundé 1 (1990-94). Senior Research Fellow (NHS) at the University of York (1979-92) and Visiting Professor, Queens University, Belfast (1984-92).

Paul Crosby is Head of Professional Practice at the AA. He qualified in 1987 after having studied architecture at Canterbury and PCL, now University of Westminster. He has held senior positions in the offices of Zaha Hadid, David Chipperfield and Martha Schwartz. He has extensive, international experience of running projects and includes setting up and running an office in Leipzig, Germany. He consults established as well as upcoming design studios on all aspects of running a practice. He has a particular research interest in the role of an architect and the nature of future practice.

Sara Grahn, Architect SAR/MSA, Professor in Sustainable Design at the School of Architecture, Royal Institute of Technology and partner at White arkitekter. Sara has extensive experience from complex assignments with an emphasis in office projects, public buildings, urban design and education. The projects are characterized by a sustainable approach, where environmental, economic and social aspects are an integral part of the architectural design. Sara's strategic and creative ability is well-documented through prizes in a number of competitions won against the highest competition standards. White arkitekter is one of Scandinavia's leading architectural practices and the 3rd largest in Europe, with over 700 employees. The practice delivers cutting-edge expertise as a result from combining academic and practice based architecture research. For White, houses, landscapes, rooms, furniture, streets and districts provide the framework for a sustainable lifestyle. Good architecture makes people grow.

Hi-VIS is open to all those who identify as women, and appreciate/understand/want to better understand/harness the latent agency and control that design (and the often dominant presence of able-bodied white middle-class men within its constituent professions) brings to bear on our environment. Our soft manifesto follows a number of Feminist design co-operatives set up in the 1980s and works towards the following: 1. Creation and upkeep of a wide network of women in Building Environment - 2. Changing the narrow definition of who & what an architect is/looks like/does - 3. Building buildings that work better for women - 4. Helping others to do the above point 3. better through disseminating research and design guides - 5. Be together, listen to each other, define a new culture for architecture, build together.

www.twitter.com/hiviscollective?lang=en

www.facebook.com/groups/hivisdesigncollective/

Thomas Hoffmann-Kuhnt was born in Wiesbaden, Germany, in 1944. After completing his apprenticeship as architectural draughtsman, he attended evening classes and got his university entrance diploma. He graduated in architecture at the Technical University of Munich. While still studying, he founded the publishing company, wa wettbewerbe aktuell in 1971, where he is still publisher and editor-in-chief. After the publishing company moved to Freiburg in the early 1990s, subsequently the wa-online presence was expanded; and the program has also been extended by the important series of wa-special topic books.

Cilly Jansen studied history of architecture at the University of Amsterdam. Since then she works in the field of art and architecture. In 1993 she founded Architectuur Lokaal, independent national centre of expertise and information devoted to commissioning building development in The Netherlands. Within this organization in 1997 she founded the Fulcrum for Procurement & Design Competitions. Since 1986 she is involved in architect selections and architecture prizes in The Netherlands and Flanders (presidency, jury member, procedures); she lectures in The

Netherlands and abroad on public commissioning and architecture policy and she was editor in chief of the *Architectuur Lokaal quarterly* 1993-2013.

Peter Wynne Rees CBE DSc HC, BSc, BArch, BTP, FRIBA, FRTPI, FRSA Professor of Places and City Planning, UCL Faculty of the Built Environment. As City Planning Officer for the City of London, Peter led the planning and regeneration of this world business and financial centre from 1985 to 2014. He lectures internationally; advises developers and cities around the world on urban planning and design; and makes frequent media appearances on these topics. Peter was the subject of a BBC profile on *The Culture Show* and was included in the Debrett's 500 list of the most inspiring and influential people in Britain today. Numerous awards have recognised his achievements and, in 2015, he was appointed a CBE for services to architecture and town planning.

Susanna Sirefman is founder and president of Dovetail Design Strategists, the leading independent architect selection firm in the United States. Dovetail draws from a deep knowledge of the field to compile stellar architect shortlists, custom-design selection processes and help organizations prepare for programmatic growth and enhanced visibility. Dovetail provides a comprehensive range of services to educate clients on the risks and opportunities inherent in a given project, whether by developing an international architecture competition, request for proposal, interview-based search or design concept commission. Trained as an architect at the Architectural Association in London, Ms. Sirefman has written five books and numerous essays on contemporary architecture and regularly contributes to *The Wall Street Journal*. Ms. Sirefman speaks widely in professional and academic settings around the world.

Craig Stott MEng, BArch, MA, ARB, is a Project Office co-director, Architect and Senior Architecture Lecturer at the Leeds School of Architecture, Leeds Beckett University. Originally trained as a Structural Engineer, Craig's research attempts to determine the impact of 'Live' project learning within architectural education by establishing its value for both the students involved and the communities who act as client for the work undertaken. The intention is to utilise the power of student design to foster ecological and social sustainability in deprived communities through this pedagogic tool.

Stefan Thommen (Gigon & Guyer Architekten). Born in St. Gallen, Switzerland, Stefan Thommen graduated from ETH Zurich and worked with Meili + Peter, before he started working for Gigon/Guyer in 2003. At Gigon/Guyer he was overall responsible for the office high-rise Prime Tower and the annex buildings as a team manager. Since 2014 Stefan Thommen is member of the management board. As a team manager, he leads the competition unit as well as the office high-rise Andreasturm and the office building Claridenstrasse in Zurich (both completion in 2018). The architectural practice Gigon/Guyer was established in 1989 by the two partners, Annette Gigon and Mike Guyer. The office has made a name for itself with its various museums and public buildings, alongside high quality residential and office buildings. Since 2012 Annette Gigon and Mike Guyer have been Professors of Architecture and Construction at the ETH Zurich.

Cindy Walters, B Arch, RIBA, is co-founder of Walters & Cohen Architects. Born in Australia, she studied architecture in South Africa and moved to London in 1990 to work for Foster + Partners before setting up the practice with Michál Cohen in 1994. Award-winning and noted projects include Bedales School in Hampshire, the Gallery of Botanical Art at Kew Gardens, Regent High School in London, and Vajrasana Buddhist Retreat Centre in Suffolk. Current projects include a significant new building for Newnham College, Cambridge. Cindy's long-standing involvement with the RIBA Awards Group includes roles on the Lubetkin Prize jury, Stirling Prize jury, and judge for the President's Research Awards.

Simon Warren BAHons, Dip, ARB, RIBA, FRSA is a Project Office co-director, Architect and Senior Architecture Lecturer at the Leeds School of Architecture, Leeds Beckett University where he leads the Post Graduate Diploma in Architectural Professional Practice (RIBA/ARB Part 3) course. A practitioner since 1992, Simon has been involved in built projects across the north of England and was a director at Leeds practice

Bauman Lyons Architects. Simon is currently working towards a PhD titled 'Live Project Pedagogy - Architecture in the Making'.

Jonathan B. Wimpenny AIA RIB. Jonathan is a registered architect in the US (NY) and the UK and is President Emeritus of the Royal Institute of British Architects USA. As a practicing architect, he has also held academic posts at the Architectural Association (London), the University of Udine (Italy) and Parsons School of Design (New York) and served on student jury panels at Bennington College (Vermont), the Art Institute (Chicago) and Columbia University (Graduate School of Architecture Planning and Preservation) as well as lecturing on architecture and city planning in Beijing (China), London (UK), Madrid (Spain), New Orleans, Denver, Chicago and New York. www.jonathanwimpennyarchitect.com

SPONSORING PARTNER

This book has been kindly supported by the Leeds School of Architecture, part of Leeds Beckett University.

The Leeds School of Architecture operates within the School of Art, Architecture & Design at Leeds Beckett University. The school established itself in the early 1900s and continues to go from strength, to strength, providing an ideal environment for the development of critical and collaborative practices in architecture.

Based in the award-winning Broadcasting Place at our university's city campus, the school prides itself on providing an environment in which its students and professionals can work together and learn from one another.

Leeds Beckett University's origins can be traced back as far as 1824. The university currently has over 28,000 students and 3,000 staff. It is estimated that over £520m of economic activity within the region is dependent on the university's teaching, research and other activities.

The Leeds Beckett School of Art, Architecture and Design has a history that spans over 170 years, and is united by a common goal: to encourage individuality, to inspire creativity, and to create impact. It has an exciting and experimental approach to contemporary creative practice – set in the heart of a culturally energised city. The school's aim is to instil all students with the confidence, curiosity and commitment to thrive at university and beyond, and to give them the freedom and independence both to think, and to make. It is more than a school, it is a community of creators and collaborators; a community nurtured by practising academic staff, many of whom are researchers of national or international standing.

The Leeds School of Architecture dates back to 1906 and delivers a variety of architectural and landscape courses that are accredited or approved by professional bodies such as the Royal Institute of British Architects, the Commonwealth Association of Architects, the Landscape Institute and the Royal Town Planning Institution.

LEEDS
BECKETT
UNIVERSITY

Hélène Lipstadt

Using the idea that architecture competitions resemble a grid as their implied organising principle, the editors of this collection aim to explore, and in so doing extend, the meaning of architecture competitions as experiments. They take the notion beyond the consensually agreed upon sense proposed (*mea culpa*, by this author)[1] of the competition as a structure, an experiment-like process, with rules that assure that results are comparable to each other, and which hints at the associated belief that the end result will not only be the selection of a superior project but also an experimental one, with all the nuances of innovation and invention that implies.

The extension is done in many ways. First and foremost, the editors add what the original definition left out: the effects — psychological, corporeal, emotional, intellectual, economic, etc — of the *experience* of participating in the *experiment*. They bring both British and international examples of the latter into counterpoint with several varieties of experimentation generated by different regulatory settings in use today, as well as with a few (and in this historian's opinion, extremely well chosen) examples of past understandings of the concept. Second, they introduce new tools of assessment that, experts in their use tell us, facilitate submission and judging, and thus the experience of participants, while bringing architecture competitions closer than ever to scientific experimentation's objective of obtaining results that are certifiably valid. Third, they open the metaphoric floor to the voices of competitions' organisers and entrants, who recount their experiences with (and within) the grid. Their tales come from points in the grid as different as competitions in the metropolises of New York, London and the school studio. A great deal of information is provided, and the offer made most engagingly. No one will come away without learning something new.

So, what is the competition grid? The metaphor is apt, if we consider the meanings associated with the terms *being on or off the grid*. Writing informally, I would define *being on the grid* as being under the influence of its energy. This is the case where national regulations or historical traditions (or both) favour or require competitions under certain conditions. It is also the case of the experience of all those who are able to engage in competing for the personal pleasure and extended educational opportunities competitions offer.

Another meaning of being *on the grid* is being active on social networking sites. Those who enter competitions are on such a grid, for competitions create networks of communication and exchange within teams and with teams' adversaries – whether these are unknown to them, as in an open competition (and therefore merely imagined), or in some phases and structures, intentionally identified by the organisers to each other. Organisers, members of the professional organisations and jurors are on that grid, as are, occasionally, stakeholders – from individuals and communities

invited to give an opinion on the impact of the competition brief on their lives to, as described here, the mayor of a great metropolis. The competition preparation process is an intensified form of the social networking present in all design preparation in a firm or studio. Even when an entry is designed autonomously, one is networking in one's head with past and recent projects for pertinent sites and briefs. In that case, one can acquire as friends (in the social networking sense of the word) any designer whose entry in a competition is known from the historical or physical record, beginning with Brunelleschi in Florence.

It is, of course, always possible *to go off the grid* in competitions, to use the term for cutting oneself off from the internet temporarily to work uninterruptedly, or from the electrical grid in order to survive entirely from one's own resources. Some of the authors would suggest that going off the competition grid is advantageous for entities searching for a designer, and for designers, because the cost of drawing on the competition grid's energy is so high, and the objective amount of power so unpredictably and randomly delivered. Unlike the colloquial meaning, *going off the competition grid* does not make one necessarily untraceable or out of range. In architecture, the amount of energy distributed by a competition grid is so immense that it can be accessed without having an official presence on it. Connections are made beforehand through collegial and classroom gossip about who is, or who is not, competing or judging, as well as afterwards through exhibitions, publications, and since 2008, the new collaborative scientific research.

The competition is also a grid in another sense. It can be understood as the fixed plane on which dynamic competitive relations play out over time, and through many moves, until there is a winner. This is the grid similar to American football's gridiron. Several references in the book to 'the rules of the game' invite us to consider that meaning, and to play with the many conceptual consequences of the metaphor.

Finally, and arguably most comprehensively, the idea of the competition grid captures the relational structure of the competition, its similarity to a force field that is analogous to a magnetic field. So many are the relational forces in our force field – with innumerable variations and yet so many regularities which have endured (thus an experimental tradition is not an oxymoron) – that the subject needs to be located and mapped, that is to say, *gridded*, time and again. This needs to be done from the many potential points of view within it – views on (and from) the dynamic relational shifting along the axes of the grid, and views of the grid as a whole, in keeping with its nature as a magnetic field.

This book does just that. Examples of the forces, and their effects in both the past and present, are very well described, producing, for this reader, an exhilarating read.

1 Hélène Lipstadt, 'Experimenting with The Experimental Tradition, 1989–2009: On Competitions and Architecture Research', in *The Architectural Competition: Research Inquiries and Experiences*, eds Magnus Rönn et al. (Stockholm: Axl Books, 2010), 58–65.

ARCHITECTURE COMPETITIONS: BETWEEN EXPERIENCE AND EXPERIMENT

Maria Theodorou and Antigoni Katsakou

In 1810, a newspaper competition for the design of Bedlam, the 'hospital' for the insane, was announced in the city of London. Among the 33 competition entries was one submitted by James Tilly Matthews, a Bedlam inmate of 14 years, who was not to be released from the hospital until his death in 1815. This one-off competition is well documented; it provides a wealth of historical information as to the use of competitions at the beginning of the 19th century for an important public building in London, and offers a glimpse into the internal politics of competitions at that time, ie who could participate, and who could win.

Matthews' entry consisted of 'a set of architecture plans, watercolour impressions and about fifty pages of notes covered in a tiny immaculate handwriting'.[1] Unsurprisingly, Matthews' entry didn't win, but he was offered £30 *ex gratia* for his designs. The first prize was awarded to one of the juror's students. None of the awarded entries was deemed suitable for construction, and thus James Lewis (the juror mentioned above) was then commissioned to combine the best ideas of all submitted designs. Surprisingly, Matthews was not an architect; he was just a self-trained draughtsman. In his endless hours of confinement, his doctor encouraged him to produce drawings of the 'air-loom machine',[2] the obsession that had him incarcerated in Bedlam in the first place. It was the competition that triggered Matthews' interest in architecture; he went on to compose a series of volumes entitled *Useful*

Architecture. A copy of the first volume was later discovered and acquired by the famous architect Sir John Soane, and is now a part of its museum collection.

Several cliches about architecture competitions seem to be already at work in this case: first, the competition was deemed appropriate because the client (the Bedlam governors) had difficulties in figuring out what they wanted, since replacing the old building 'demanded a vision for the care of the insane'[3] – and it was thought best to collect ideas by launching an open invitation to whomever wanted to contribute. Second, an interesting entry – although not the first prize winner – gave its designer a chance to 'make a name', or perhaps it is better to say, 'opened his way' into architecture.

There is, however, something far more interesting in the Bedlam case study, for it unravels the setting up of the institution of architecture competitions within the framework of 19th-century scientific thinking around 'experimentation'. Since this book's focus is on the concept and practice of 'experimentation' in architecture competitions, it is worth exploring this to fully grasp the event formation of experimentation. An informed reader, together with the book's contributors, can then reflect on experimentation's current facets, effects or even usefulness in architectural competitions.

A pertinent question would be the following: Why (and how) was it possible for an incurable lunatic, who remains in the history of psychiatric diagnosis as the first case of paranoid schizophrenia,[4] to be considered 'eligible' to enter an architecture competition? The question could be slightly tweaked in order to provide clues for answering it: How could a set of architectural drawings and a text of recommendations that were the translation of an inmate's first-hand experience of the asylum be used as an eligible entry to an architecture competition?

The answer is provided by the relation between experience and experiment. In fact, this relation is at the very core of 19th-century scientific thought. Bruno Latour[5] discusses the difference between 'being experienced' and being an 'experimenter'. In the former, skill, knowledge and know-how is embodied in the very flesh of the experienced person. The experience is turned into material upon which to experiment, once it is recorded and shared in places where similar experiences are gathered and combined. In the latter, instead of being *in*corporated, skill, knowledge and know-how is *ex*corporated: it is inscribed into drawings, charts and papers which become accessible and ready to be used. It is through this process that the sedimentation of experiences in a body gets transformed into a 'body of knowledge' available to experimentation, and experiences become a collection of 'objects' offered and open to experiment.

Matthews *excorporated* his individual experience by turning it into architectural blueprints and a text available for others to view, read, comment upon, assess, reuse, study and store, etc. By entering the competition, he could prove he was more than just an inmate of the building (the asylum) experiencing the effects of confinement and treatments. He was in fact able to turn the experience inscribed onto his body into a set of observations.[6] Noted down, distanced from his own body, the material Matthews produced became a 'body of knowledge' on which he could experiment by drafting an architectural proposal; drawings and writing could thus be communicated to others for validation and approval. From experience to experiment, a way was paved from paranoia (seclusion in one's own mind) to the sanity of being able to communicate with others by the means and rituals of an ideas-led architecture competition. And Matthews partially succeeded in his experimentation – although the reasons for his confinement were far more complex. Such was the relation between experience and experiment at the eve of scientific thinking that Matthews himself became an object of study and experimentation for his doctor.[7]

The relation between experience and experiment seems faded or forgotten after so many years of operating within the scientific mindset; then again, it may have been altered but still present, though not visible.

Experimentation in architecture competitions is usually understood in relation to the outcome – the experimental architectural object or project; or it refers to the structure of the architectural competition itself.[8] In the latter, a strict framework of processes – which includes regulations, evaluation criteria and other protocols to be followed – secures a laboratory-like setting in which architects can experiment. This understanding of experimentation follows the 19th-century scientific framework which was produced as a process of *excorporation*. By revisiting the almost forgotten relation of experiment to experience, this book aims to bring into the discussion the complexity of embodied practices involved in the process of experimenting with, and within, architecture competitions.

Generations of architects have experienced what entering architecture competitions feels like – excitement, exhaustion, frustration, jubilation and disappointment – and their corporeal effects have been inscribed on their bodies and brains time and again with the intensity of experimenting with ideas to convey and excel. However, these experiences have very rarely been approached as an object of study. Competitions' material has accumulated, although in large part it has remained inaccessible. Nonetheless, slowly and surely, researchers – the International Network of Researchers on Competitions is one example[9] – are approaching architecture competitions as a research topic. Competitions are becoming an emerging field of research, their processional framework and structure being put under scrutiny, recorded, archived and analysed, their effects being criticised, and their potential being discussed to identify further developments.

This book brings together these two, apparently different, strands: on the one hand, it reviews architectural competitions as experienced by those who participate in them; on the other, it examines how competitions are used as arenas of experimentation within the laboratory-like setting of the competitions' institution of regulated processes.[10] The aim of the book is to bridge these strands by combining a series of essays with discussions, involving a variety of actors and practitioners, in the UK and internationally.

In each of the book's four themed sections, three essays drafted by a variety of authors are counterpoised with a set of discussions between the editors and practitioners involved in competitions in different capacities. The choice of discussants was strategic, and aimed to describe the range of architecture competition experiences. Interviewees were not drawn exclusively from the obvious 'class' of practitioners who experienced competitions when putting forward experimental ideas on sites and building tasks. The editors thought that different categories of actors had interesting stories to tell, and they interviewed expert consultants involved in the organisation of competitions, jury members who validate and assess competition entries, architecture editors who select and present competitions to the public, as well as commissioners and client advisers, who join in to create expectation standards from the competitions' process framework. The editors were particularly interested to address gender issues within the context of architecture competitions' institution and practices, and in the concept of experimentation produced within the scientific framework. The selection of contributors reflects not only a numeric gender-balanced approach but also allows for gender concerns to be articulated in the essays and the discussions.

Part 1, which has more of an introductory nature, paves the way for Parts 2 and 3, where the discussion on experimentation broadens geographically and thematically. Part 4 offers additional 'food for thought' in terms of the social and political potential of architectural competitions.

Looking now in more detail, Part 1 focuses on the institution of competition and its set-up as a laboratory for experimentation, exploring what has been the role of architects' professional organisations in shaping competitions' process framework. Judith Strong gives an informed and up-to-date overview of RIBA's role in regulating competitions, while Aymone Nicolas offers a snapshot of the past with a historical account of the International Union of Architects' (*Union Internationale des Architectes*, UIA) international competition politics in the crucial decades of reconstruction after the Second World War. Elisabeth Tostrup dissects the rhetorical tropes generated within competitions and reveals how 'representation' is inextricably linked with the scientific frame of experimentation; her text addresses the politics of design through the analysis of its power of communication and persuasion.

Two discussions counterbalance the scholarly essays by bringing back the immediacy of 'presence' that experience entails. Paul Crosby describes his role as director of competitions at David Chipperfield's office, using his experience to analyse (and make suggestions for strengthening) RIBA's role in organising competitions. Part 1 concludes with a set of discussants all involved in RIBA-USA competitions: Angela Brady OBE, Jonathan Wimpenny, Tim Clark and Phil Allsopp recount (and reflect upon) their experimentations with the competition format and content, to address social, cultural, political and environmental issues.

In Part 2, Kristian Kreiner, Magnus Rönn, Leentje Volker and Marina Bos-de Vos expand our knowledge of how competitions' institutions operate in three European countries: Denmark, Sweden and the Netherlands. These countries have a strong tradition of state-regulated architectural procurement by experimenting *within* competitions. Kristian Kreiner discusses the ongoing experimentation with different competition formats and procedures in the Danish context, while wondering whether experimentation can be limited to these aspects only. Magnus Rönn focuses on competitions validated by Architects Sweden to tease out factors and actors (such as clients) that could potentially encourage innovation in architecture competitions. Leentje Volker and Marina Bos-de Vos highlight current managerial trends, and their not-always-positive impact on Dutch architectural competition culture; their essay touches on the burning question of whether architects' compensation is both sufficient and efficient incentive for participating in competitions.

In the discussion section of Part 2, the voices of practitioners and representatives of acclaimed architectural firms in the UK and abroad narrate their first-hand experiences with architectural competitions. Sara Grahn (White Arkitekter, Sweden), Stefan Thommen (Gigon/Guyer, Switzerland), Angel Borrego Cubero (OSS, Spain) and Cindy Walters (Walters & Cohen, UK) reflect on the ways competitions may influence and forge architects' professional

5

careers, in their own countries and internationally. They discuss the design of competition entries, comment on the instructive power that competitions hold for young architects, and offer their practice-based advice. The direct juxtaposition of their answers to the editors' inquiry puts into the spotlight the range of their competition-related experiences and accumulated knowledge, which is eventually reflected in each distinct design approach and the apprehension of architecture itself.

Part 3 provides an opportunity to explore the future of competitions as it examines the application of new technologies as a potential field for experimenting *with* architecture competitions. The implications of e-procurement, in both the European and British context, are discussed by Walter Menteth. The application of Building Information Modelling (BIM) as a requirement in competition entries is presented, in the context of the Norwegian experience, by Birgitte Sauge; she feeds the debate on the additional workload that current technological advancements may entail for competition submissions, as well as on the evaluation criteria applied in their case. Tiina Merikoski uses a case study from Finland to argue that digital tools, which decode the representational languages of the visual material submitted as part of competition entries, can assist jurors in their assessment. Her essay reminds the reader that objective truth and validation of results has always been (and still is) at the heart of any scientific experiment; whether this framework can be adopted in the competitions' canvas nonetheless remains open to discussion. Both Merikoski and Sauge tackle the discourse around the commensurability of competition proposals, and the evaluation frame of architectural quality that competition juries are called to put into action.

First-hand competition experiences are still at the heart of the discussion at the end of Part 3, although in this case through a distinct lens that counterbalances the accounts of Part 2. Tom Bloxham represents Urban Splash, a major British developer firm; Cilly Jansen and Susanna Sirefman represent their respective organisations for architects' selection, competition organisation and public commissioning in the Netherlands and United States; finally, Thomas Hoffmann-Kuhnt represents the German *wettbewerbe aktuell*, one of the most accredited European magazines specialising in the topic of competitions, of which he is editor-in-chief. Together they offer accounts of the initiation of competition procedures and of the commissioners' expectations of them. They comment upon the architectural quality of competition submissions, while their stories – once more directly juxtaposed as alternated answers to the editors' query – offer clues regarding the shifting ground of competitions in current practice.

In Part 4, essay authors revisit and rethink the structures and formats of competitions. Jeremy Till provides a critique of the institution of competitions, and points to its political aspects rather than its internal politics; he argues for a much needed (if not already happening) socio-political and financial shift, and considers its reverberations on the institution of competitions. Robert Hammond, on the other hand, reflects on the impact of the first and second High Line competitions in New York, which he conceived and implemented. The success of this project radically altered the area to the point that Robert, co-founder and executive director of the Friends of The High Line organisation, considers community input and engagement to be paramount in making the project socially sustainable. The historical focus of Florian Kossak's essay unravels the 1970s socio-political context; he presents the processes and the effects of a highly successful community-engaging experiment in the case of the Kreuzberg competition in Berlin. History in the scientific frame provides a provides a better grasp of the present and should not be confused with historicism in which the past is applied to the present.

The discussion in Part 4 includes Peter Wynne Rees's experience as a chief planner of the City of London, which led him to distrust competitions for architecture procurement. Interestingly, he points to the difference between scientific experiments and laboratory testing, and the 'messy' production of architecture, in which experiments can lead to disappointing, even disastrous, outcomes. Educators Simon Warren and Craig Stott discuss the process of *excorporating* the competition experience of architecture students, so that it becomes validated, and part of their academic education. Last but not least, the Hi-VIS Feminist Design Collective's polemical text powerfully closes Part 4, forcing the reader to confront the side-effects of competitions. The collective both recounts and reflects upon how procedures and implicit rules get imprinted onto the bodies of architects, especially the bodies of those who belong to the non-hegemonic categories of gender. A polemic is not a scientifically valid way of reasoning; in it, chunks of experience are used to challenge the familiar and customary, and as such pave the way for experimenting differently.

The reader of this book is invited to consider various aspects, and sometimes conflicting views, of experiences and arguments on architecture competitions, and challenged to think them through. Moreover, by merging the tropes of scientific writing with the immediacy of practitioners' direct competition experiences and stories, the book aims to be accessible, informative and enjoyable – to both the academic readership and professionals of the field. Although the book does not promise to help professionals win competitions, it does make the behind-the-scenes operations of competitions visible, and can perhaps entice professionals to turn their own experiences into a body of knowledge with which they can experiment further. To the academic, the book offers an insight into the potential that architecture competitions hold as an emerging research field.

Notes

1   The material for the presentation of this case study is mainly drawn from Mike Jay, *The Influencing Machine: James Tilly Matthews and the Air Loom* (London: Strange Attractor Press, 2012).

2   The air loom was imagined by Matthews as a secret weapon hidden in the basement of London buildings to send gases and rays aimed at political brainwashing. Jay, *The Influencing Machine*, 48–49.

3   Jay, *The Influencing Machine*, 184.

4   Matthews' doctor, John Haslam, presented his clinical observations in his book, *Illustrations of Madness*, and made James Tilly Matthews the first case study in the history of modern diagnosis of paranoid schizophrenia. See also note 7.

5   Bruno Latour, 'The Force and Reason of Experiment', in *Experimental Inquiries*, ed. Homer Le Grand (Dordrecht: Kluwer Academic Publishers, 1990), 49–80.

6   'An observation is an experiment where the body of the scientist is used as an instrument, complete with its writing device, that is, a hand, a quill and a notebook', Bruno Latour, 'The Force and Reason of Experiment', 56.

7   The daily experience of the doctor with this patient was turned into observation, detailed descriptions and other material, which were transcribed into a book that now belongs to the history of psychiatry. In the process, the scientific approach to 'mental conditions' was to transform the asylum into the architecture typology of the psychiatric hospital.

8   Hélène Lipstadt, 'The Experimental Tradition', in *The Experimental Tradition: Essays on Competitions in Architecture*, ed. Hélène Lipstadt (New York: Princeton Architectural Press, 1989), 9–20.

9   The International Network of Researchers on Competitions has already organised a series of conferences in various countries. The most recent one, the 6th International Conference on Competitions, was organised by the editors of this book in 2016 at the School of Architecture, Leeds Beckett University, UK. http://www.leedsbeckett.ac.uk/icc2016/.

10 Bechara Helal describes the setting up of scientific processes, including laboratories which create and secure the conditions for scientific experimentation, and points out similarities and differences in processes followed in architecture competitions to allow experimentation. Bechara Halal, 'Competitions as Laboratories', in *Architecture Competitions and the Production of Culture, Quality and Knowledge: An International Inquiry*, eds Jean-Pierre Chupin, Carmela Cucuzzella and Bechara Helal (Montreal: Potential Architecture Books, 2015), 232–253.

PROJECT N° 014

ECHELLE 1:2500

1ST PRIZE

M. JEAN TSCHUMI, LAU

PART

CHAPTER 1

THE EVOLUTION OF THE UK COMPETITION SYSTEM

Judith Strong

Introduction

Founded in 1834, the Royal Institute of British Architects (RIBA) was one of the earliest professional architectural associations, and one of the first to seek to regulate the way its members competed for work. The foundations for what is often described as the traditional architectural competition can be traced back to the rules drawn up by the RIBA Council at the beginning of the last century.

The UK, however, has never developed a competition culture comparable with those of many other European countries, and no UK legislation exists, now or in the past, requiring architects for public buildings to be appointed through a formal competition procedure. Repeated attempts to promote open design competitions have met with limited success. Over the years, advocates of the competition system have increasingly had to rely more on persuasion than control.

This essay looks at the factors which have impacted the way architects and design teams are selected and appointed, and how they have changed the way competitions are organised in the UK. It describes recent initiatives to promote a more flexible system, while retaining the safeguards for architects, clients and the public that the more formal structures aim to secure.

Early attempts to regulate competitive work

The practice of asking a number of architects to submit plans and drawings before being awarded a commission is certainly not a new phenomenon. In the UK, more than 2,500 competitions were held between 1850 and 1900, producing numerous prestigious buildings, but doing so in an atmosphere of increasing controversy, with accusations of incompetence and general corruption being levelled at both clients and competing architects. In 1880, a petition[1] was drawn up asking the RIBA Council to devise a remedy, its 1,300 signatories pledging refusal to participate in any competition without a professional adviser. In 1907, a regulatory system was introduced requiring qualified assessment, reasonable rewards and a commitment to the winner. RIBA members were prohibited from responding to invitations to submit designs in any competition which did not follow these rules.

Throughout the following 110 years, government legislation, initiatives and lobby groups within the design and construction industries, as well as the procurement directives introduced by the European Union, have all had their effect on how clients procure design services, and how architects compete for work in the UK. During the first half of the last century, the profession tightened its grip on competitive work. Regulations were introduced requiring the promoter to appoint an all-architect jury nominated by the president of RIBA, and to build the design that the jury recommended (or pay compensation of 1.5% of the estimated building cost). These restrictions tended to deter clients from opting for the competition system, but the way the architectural profession was structured also played a role. When building work resumed after the Second World War, commissions tended to go to the larger, more established practices, or be carried out 'in house' by public and local authority architects' departments. To give one example, the Royal Festival Hall (1951) and adjacent arts buildings on the South Bank of the river Thames (opened 1967) in London were all designed by specialist teams within the former London County Council architects' department.

Elsewhere in Europe, the system was being more widely used, with many of the buildings which resulted from competitions being featured in design magazines. Inspired by these examples, a group of architects began to push RIBA to revise its rules and to promote the competition system in order to provide opportunities for younger members of the profession, and to raise the quality of what was being designed and built. Towards the end of the 1960s, RIBA drew up a new set of regulations[2] and standard conditions giving clients a greater role in the competition process, but with architects forming the majority of the selection panel, anonymity closely protected, and the architects of the winning design being appointed for the commission (or paid standard fees for the work already undertaken). The documentation was picked up by the UIA and applied to the international competition system.[3]

Quality assurance was overseen by RIBA, which would only approve competitions that followed its regulations, including the use of standard forms of conditions setting out the terms of appointment. The process, however, was dependent on RIBA having control over the way architects sought commissions, and how they charged for their services. Speculative design work was prohibited; if clients wanted to look at how different architects might approach a problem, they had to pay each of them the standard fee for the work or promote an approved architectural competition.

Government interventions weaken RIBA control

Everything changed in the 1980s when the Thatcher government,[4] committed to the concept of a market-led economy, started to look at what it regarded as the protective practices of professional institutions. Increasing pressure from both the Monopolies and Mergers Commission and the Office of Fair Trading meant that RIBA initially lost its control over members competing for work, and subsequently abandoned any attempt to maintain even a recommended fee scale. Clients were free to define their own procurement systems – including the system of fee bidding.

Many more clients chose to organise procedures requiring outline designs to be submitted. While some were well run and produced good results, others were less satisfactory. Common failings included inadequate preparation and poor briefing, lack of relevant expertise on selection panels, demands for excessive amounts of work for little or no payment, and no guarantee that the architect would be appointed to take his or her design through to completion. All such projects tended to be labelled as competitions by the media, regardless of whether they followed recommended processes or not, and this led to unwarranted criticisms of the approved competition system, and a reluctance by many in the architectural profession to see an increase in its use.

The perceived difficulties were highlighted by the introduction of the National Lottery[5] in 1994. Initially, much of the money raised was earmarked for capital projects, with a number of distributing bodies being appointed from within the charity, heritage, arts and sport sectors to oversee the process. Arts England, which had 'quality of architecture' within its remit, pushed for all lottery projects to be the subject of architectural competitions, the other distributing bodies followed suit. The amount of money being invested during a time of relative recession within the construction industry meant that a significant proportion of the architectural profession looked to secure commissions to design lottery-funded projects.

The impact of EU procurement legislation

By chance, the launch of the National Lottery coincided with the issue of EU procurement directives which extended jurisdiction from goods to services – including the services of architects and the design team professions. These directives[6] covered contracts entered into by public bodies or projects funded in whole or in part (over 50%) from public sources. The rules came into effect when a commission passed a given threshold figure. The vast majority of lottery projects relied on putting together funding packages from a variety of publicly financed organisations, which meant that most commissions would have needed to follow EU procurement rules.

When the EU directives were first introduced, they identified three basic formats: open, restricted or (in limited circumstances) negotiated. Contracts were to be advertised and selection made against published criteria, with the emphasis being placed on 'the most economically advantageous'. A fourth route was to hold a 'design contest', organised along the lines of the traditional architectural competition system prevalent in much of Europe.

Unlike many EU countries, the UK had still not been able to establish a competition culture, and public bodies were wary of making appointments 'unseen', ie on the basis of the designs alone. They wanted assurances about the capability and compatibility of those who would work with them to deliver the projects. 'In the UK the emphasis for the majority of projects is for contracting authorities to select an architect with whom they can work effectively.'[7] At the same time, architects feared that a requirement for design contests to be mandatory would lead to unsustainable levels of unpaid design works. But they were also worried by the alternatives offered by the EU, believing that the term 'economically advantageous' would lead to an escalation in fee bidding.

Introducing interviews into the competition system

In response, the RIBA Council sought to bring in a selection procedure which would respond to the lottery-distributing bodies' desire for competitions, limit the demands on the profession, avoid simple fee bidding, and meet the requirements set by the EU directives. The aim was to 'provide clients with a comparatively fast, inexpensive and efficient method of selecting a design team by means of competition'. What emerged was the 'competitive interview'.[8] There was no question of anonymity or a requirement for an independent jury, although it was recommended that a professional adviser be appointed to guide the client. Prizes and 'honoraria' (discretionary payments) were only given when design work was required.

The system came to be used either for selecting an architect/design team for appointment or for shortlisting applicants before asking a small number to prepare designs, the latter process effectively replacing the initial design-based selection stage of a traditional two-stage competition.

It worked as follows:

- *Advertise to invite Expressions of Interest (EOIs), providing an outline brief, establishing the criteria for selection, and specifying the information to be submitted.*

- *Draw up an initial shortlist on the basis of the information submitted in response.*

- *Organise interviews at which each of the shortlisted teams is required to make a presentation outlining its approach and demonstrating the expertise available within the team.*

- *Draw up a more detailed brief and ask a limited number to prepare designs.*

Various other techniques have been introduced as part of both the briefing and selection processes, including guided site visits, open question-and-answer sessions, visits to buildings and architects' offices, discussions with previous clients, community workshops and wider-ranging seminars. While this more flexible approach suited many clients and produced good outcomes, there were very few competitions organised according to design contest rules. The open competition was also a rarity. A report[9] on trends in the procurement of design services states that there were only two open competitions held during the years 2008–14, although this figure may refer solely to competitions which were subject to EU procurement rules.

When introduced, the RIBA competitive interview and its variations were seen as falling within the EU 'restricted' designation. In 2004, at the instigation of the UK government, the EU added the 'competitive dialogue',[10] designated as an alternative to the negotiated procedure which it has subsequently largely replaced.

PQQs and quantitative scoring

The process of shortlisting for interview took the UK system out of the competitions procedures of the design contest into the more standard EU procurement legislation. Methodologies which could be considered appropriate for the commissioning of specific goods or services were increasingly being used to select or pre-select architects. Criteria tended to be weighted towards the quantitative rather than the qualitative, ie areas that could be easily scored rather than those which required informed judgment in order to make an assessment. Size of practice, turnover, range of similar projects completed, number of qualified staff, and levels of professional indemnity insurance all tended to be prioritised. Respondents to invitations to tender were required to complete Pre-Qualification Questionnaires (PQQs), which often included a requirement for detailed statements to be submitted demonstrating compliance with government employment policies. These statements were also assessed and awarded marks for 'good practice'.

The combination of quantitative scoring and time-consuming PQQs led to shortlists which were concentrated on the larger, more established practices. A report published in 2014[11] notes that 97% of all UK practices are small or medium-sized enterprises (SMEs) and 79% employ ten or fewer people. The report comments: 'One result of the current procurement system is that much of the UK's talent is locked out of the market or discouraged from tendering.' This meant, in effect, that many of the key arguments for the competition system – exploring different approaches, spreading opportunities more widely across the profession, and discovering and encouraging new talent – were being lost as the competitive interview system became more widely used.

Rediscovering the value of open design competitions

Over the last few years, RIBA has begun both to address these problems and to make efforts to encourage clients to consider more open competition procedures, including those which select predominantly on the basis of the quality of the designs submitted.

In 2012, a report was commissioned to be submitted to the government entitled *Building Ladders of Opportunity: How Reforming Construction Procurement Can Drive Growth in the UK Economy*. The main report contained a number of points relating to the need to simplify the procurement procedures (including PQQs),[12] and concluded with three sets of key recommendations. The third set focused on creating 'a competitive market by increasing access and allowing the public sector to take full advantage of UK design talent', and included the specific recommendation that 'The Government should work with RIBA to promote and improve the use of design Competitions.'[13]

For many years, RIBA's Competitions Office had promoted its fee-earning management service, but had not offered any general guidance to clients as to how competitions should be run. This shows signs of changing. In 2012, RIBA published *Design Competitions Guidance for Clients*, setting out RIBA best practice standards.[14] The document does not set out rules to be followed but provides a guide to the competition system and explains the principles on which it is based. It illustrates this with examples of successful projects, detailing the benefits and giving practical information on potential problems, and how they are best avoided. A useful chart is included, giving an overview of the various formats within RIBA's competition system.

In order to further the process of reappraisal, a task force was convened in 2013, comprising clients, architects, client advisers and competition organisers,[15] with the remit of reviewing the value of architectural competitions in the UK.

Their report concludes with a series of recommendations under the following five headings:

1. *Celebrate and promote the benefits of competitions for all types of buildings and structures.*

2. *Increase the quantity of well-managed, well-regulated competitions.*

3. *Provide new best practice guidance and support to clients (building on the 2012 RIBA **Design Competitions Guidance for Clients** document).*

4. *Promote best practice and continuous improvement to processes.*

5. *Influence the standards of other competition providers and private clients working in partnership with other professional associations.*

This new focus on promoting the competition system more actively appears to be meeting with some success. The number of competitions run by RIBA and other competent managers is increasing, and there are also more open competitions. Special buildings and projects still tend to dominate and attract media coverage, but one of the aims of RIBA is to extend the use of the system to what the task force describes as the 'beautiful ordinary'.[16]

A new guidance document[17] was produced at the end of 2016 and is available to those registering their interest with RIBA's Competitions Office. This is supplemented by *RIBA Competitions Guidance for Competition Entrants*,[18] RIBA's first competition documentation to be directed specifically at architects and design teams.

Notes

1 'Architectural Competitions' Memorial, 1880.

2 Included as an appendix in Judith Strong, *Participating in Architectural Competitions: A Guide for Competitors, Promoters and Assessors* (London: Architectural Press, 1976).

3 *Ibid.*

4 The government headed by Margaret Thatcher, 1979–1990.

5 The National Lottery Act 1993; on this subject see also Judith Strong, *Winning by Design: Architectural Competitions* (Oxford: Butterworth-Heinemann, 1996), 93–102.

6 The Public Services Contracts Regulations 1993 (SI 1993/3228), Directives 93/36, 93/37 and 93/38.

7 Burges Salmon, *Comparative Procurement: Procurement Regulation and Practice in Germany, Sweden and the UK* (London: RIBA, 2012), 3. Available from: http://www.architecture.com http://www.architecture.com/RIBA_Comparative_procurement.pdf. Burges Salmon is an independent law firm commissioned by RIBA; the report examines the comparative implementation of the EU Public Procurement Directive Germany, Sweden and the UK.

8 The term 'competitive interview' describes an EU-compliant competitive system devised and promoted by RIBA 'to be used to select a designer and/or design team at the early stage of a project. It enables the client and the designer to develop and evolve the design together'. *Design Competitions Guidance for Clients* (London: RIBA, 2012), 8. Available online (though no longer being issued by RIBA) from: http://www.competitions.architecture. com. http:www.//competitions.architecture.com/ Doc/Guidance_For_Clients.pdf. It was originally introduced in the mid-1990s and widely used for lottery projects where an initial input was required to support bids for funding the design development.

9 Walter Menteth et al., *Public Construction Procurement Trends 2009–2014* (London: Project Compass CIC, 2014), available from: Project Compass http://www.projectcompass.co.uk/ publications/Project_Compass_CIC_Procurement_ Trends_2009-2014.pdf.

10 Directive 2004/18/EC 2006. An analysis is given in a report by Burges Salmon commissioned by RIBA which examines the comparative implementation of the EU Public Procurement Directive in Germany, Sweden and the UK.

11 Walter Menteth et al., *Public Construction Procurement Trends 2009–2014* (London: Project Compass CIC, 2014), available from: Project Compass http://www.projectcompass.co.uk/ publications/Project_Compass_CIC_Procurement_ Trends_2009-2014.pdf.

12 In October 2016, PQQs were replaced by the less onerous SQs (Standard Qualifications).

13 *Building Ladders of Opportunity: How Reforming Construction Procurement Can Drive Growth in the UK Economy* (London: RIBA, 2012), 3. Available from: Building Design online http:// www.bdonline.co.uk/Journals/2012/05/24/m/n/a/ BuildingLaddersofOpportunity.pdf.

14 *Design Competitions Guidance for Clients* (London: RIBA, 2012).

15 *A Review of Architectural Design Competitions and Other Competitive Processes by the RIBA Competitions Task Group* (London: RIBA, 2014), available from: http://www.architecture.com http://www.architecture.com/Files/ RIBAProfessionalServices/CompetitionsOffice/ CompetitionsTaskGroupReport.pdf

16 At the time of writing (November 2016), discussions regarding the future relationship between the post-Brexit UK and the EU were at a very early stage. Whether competitions will continue to be open to all architects on a reciprocal basis is a matter for speculation.

17 *RIBA Competitions Guidance for Clients 2016.* http://www.ribacompetitions.com.

18 *RIBA Competitions Guidance for Competition Entrants* (London: RIBA, 2016), available from: http://www.ribacompetitions.com/downloads/ RIBA_Competitions_Entrant_Guide.pdf.

ON COMPETITION RHETORIC AND CONTEMPORARY TRENDS

Elisabeth Tostrup

Architectural competitions are about projecting and selecting the best solution among many parallel and competing proposals to a design problem. Rhetoric, then, in a wide sense, is essential because all levels of presentation involve purposeful and persuasive (or even argumentative) discourse in which the speaker (*rhetor*), here the author or designer, deliberately attempts to bring others round to his or her way of thinking.

There is a fundamental connection between the two arts, architecture and rhetoric. As Christine Smith points out, referring to Leon Battista Alberti: 'since the purpose of architecture, as Alberti saw it, was like that of rhetoric [...] to persuade the mind of the hearer and move his emotions'.[1] This is particularly true in competitions, when the success of the winning project depends upon its capacity to convince the jury, and the wider audience, more than the other entries. To 'persuade the mind' in classical rhetoric involves informing/reason, *logos*, and delighting, that is, to appear credible, *ethos*. In order to succeed, however, the performance or submission must also 'move the emotions' of the audience, which involves the *pathos* element. These three rhetorical modes are clearly still active today, applied with the techniques and means that the participants have at their disposal within the framework of the competition.

Architectural competitions are an international phenomenon, and their procedures and prevalence may vary from country to country. The references for this text are competitions held in Norway, which after 1994 have been subject to the European Accessibility Act regulations relating to public procurement. Over the past decades, the forms of competition have become conspicuously more varied. Invited, closed competitions, for example, when anonymity is not paramount, may include videos and other kinds of personal presentations.[2] According to Ole Gustavsen, partner in the Norway-based studio Snøhetta, many competitions now are based on interviews without any design proposal.[3] Nonetheless, the concern here is the typical architectural competition, which is based on the submission of design material in accordance with specifications given in the brief, and in which anonymity is the rule. Importantly, the demands and constraints of the briefs secure submissions that are comparable, on equal terms – which is the framework for the rhetorical strategies.

Who is the competition rhetoric aimed at?

Hélène Lipstadt describes competitions as a particular field of cultural production in the Bourdieusian sense, and as such characterised by the disinterestedness of the participants: 'A competition is thus a space in which the architect can act as if, and believe themselves to be, full-fledged, relatively autonomous creators.'[4] Competitions celebrate the notion of the architect as an artist. The submissions address the inter-professional community of architects, at an idealistic level, which is detached from the client and the realisation process, and thus enjoys a certain degree of autonomy. The competition achievements are given authority in the architecture culture, a contemporary version of 'the academy' according to Barry Bergdoll.[5]

An experienced Norwegian architect jury member recently stated that laymen have a strong influence on assessment in Norwegian competitions: 'There are many voices and every voice has equal weight, whether or not they are architects, whereas in Denmark, the general respect for the architect as a professional, is greater.'[6] In the 20th century, the majority of competition jury members were normally architects. Now, juries frequently have more members, and the additional members are usually *not* architects. Architectural competitions are a public matter, and the proposals must also persuade laymen in various roles: as jury members, and in political and administrative institutions, as well as the general public. This is especially the case in projects which are subject to great public interest and debate in the media. Hence, the competition rhetoric must convince a wide and differentiated audience, which is prejudiced in terms of preconditioned skills and knowledge, desires and emotions.

Three types of rhetorical agents

Architectural proposals as rhetoric operate through three types of arguments: first, the proposed work of architecture as it is prefigured in the visual material; second, the visual representation itself as a field of rhetorical strategy; and third, the verbal material – the texts – which acts as a separate rhetorical instrument in the promotion of the competition proposals. The rhetorical character of the proposed architecture is evident, though often overlooked, if one fails to acknowledge the relativism involved in the project and considers only the presentation, 'the wrapping', to be rhetoric. A work of architecture is not objective, nor the only answer to a problem, but expresses certain value orientations, and prioritises certain qualities more than others. Every architectural project is an argument in the ongoing debate on architecture and the built environment.

The concept of 'figuration', used to differentiate representations by architects from other representations of architecture, is specific to the architect, since it signifies that the 'figurator' interposes him or herself as a scaling device between the future three-dimensional, full-scale building and the image of the building.[7] Competition projects are not working drawings but simplified provisional proposals that outline a credible figuration, a credible potential for further elaboration. Neither are they first-hand figurations used in the design process, but a presentation of these selected at a particular stage in the process, and shaped purposely for the competition audience.[8] The types of competition figurations are prescribed by the briefs, and usually follow the conventions of the architecture profession: orthogonal projections – plans, sections and elevations – and a few perspectives as well as a model of the proposed building, often to be inserted into a larger model which encompasses the built environment. Additional visual material, sketches, photographs or diagrams may normally be submitted, pasted on a limited number (usually six to eight) of plates or printed in the A3 report. These figurations and visualisations constitute the second means of rhetorical strategy in competitions. By their very nature, these miniature, simplified visualisations emphasise, exaggerate, veil and ignore certain aspects of the proposed architecture and its context.

The third rhetorical field is the textual material, which comprises the competition briefs and the architects' texts accompanying the projects, as well as the jury's final report. Together, these texts constitute a cocktail of dry/technical and stimulating/evocative verbal 'discourse of legitimation' with reference to the visual material, which is created to satisfy the three rhetorical aspects of *logos*, *ethos* and *pathos*.[9] Catchy slogans and metaphors in the texts seem to gain a status of their own as bright mental banners that symbolise the implicit lifestyle and the conceptions of use that are embodied in the proposals.[10] Combined with the tendency to repeat oneself typical of the writing of architects, these metaphors and slogans constitute the rhetorical amplification that makes the message effective.

Rather than outlining separate analyses of the three different rhetorical agents (the architecture, and the visual and verbal material), examples of all three will be treated in a joint text below. The visual material plays a leading role in the threefold competition rhetoric; it visualises the prefigured architecture, and is a reference for the verbal statements. It is on this matter that the competition rhetoric seems to have undergone the greatest change over the past decades, along with the increasing impact of visual culture.[11] The following will look in particular at contemporary trends in competition rhetoric, and also includes a historic case to demonstrate change and continuity.

Orthogonal projections – subjective objectivity

Owing to the digital revolution, competition figurations have become considerably more complex and colourful over the past decades. While the techniques have changed, conventional architectural projections – plans, sections and elevations – are still significant in competitions. Orthogonal projections are considered the most 'objective' representation, which reproduces the actual proportional relations of the object. They are essential in order for the jury to judge whether (and how) the competitor has solved the organisation of the spaces, and to see the potential for realisation. Axonometric perspectives, which also reproduce 'true' proportions, help in this respect, either to illustrate the volumes or as diagrams visualising different aspects, such as circulation.

Architects are thoroughly trained in interpreting miniature architectural figurations, and are able to conduct the visual thinking necessary to comprehend the objects in space. Because of its abstract nature and dependence on training, an 'objective' orthogonal rendering may cause greater 'subjectivity' of perception.[12] As a result, architects have an advantage over lay people when it comes to foreseeing the consequences in full-scale realisations. While they inform proportional relations in space correctly, these architectural figurations also act rhetorically, conditioned by the prevailing design modes of the time, and often without even the architects being aware of the relativism and rhetoric involved.[13]

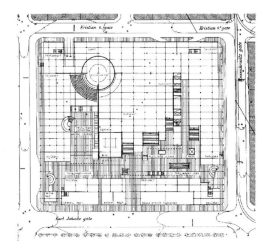

Figure 1.1a Karl Johan-kvartalet, competition drawings, motto 13831, by Håkon Mjelva, ground floor plan, published in *Norske arkitektkonkurranser* No 93, 1963

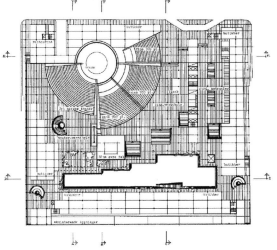

Figure 1.1b Karl Johan-kvartalet, competition drawings, motto 13831, by Håkon Mjelva, first floor plan, published in *Norske arkitektkonkurranser* No 93, 1963

For example, the plan drawings in the 1962 competition for the *Karl Johan-kvartalet*, a block on the main street of Oslo, exaggerate 'openness' and 'temporality', and display the entire complex as a continuous open space, filling out the site in a structural, 'neutral' grid (see Fig. 1.1a and Fig. 1.1b).[14] The manner in which the spatial arrangement is shaped, rather than being perceived in a state of rest, underlines the open, dynamic coherence and circulation of air and people. The shaping of the lavish passage through the block enhances the dynamic impression. The large circular shape of the theatre and cinemas, the asymmetrical open well and the excessive flight of stairs, irregularly placed, which connect the two floors with sweeping movements, become spatial focal points which are approached and passed by. In this competition, the main verbal legitimation was 'spatial liberation' in the interior, the 'enriching flow' of people from the street moving through the 'liberating total solution'. While stressing human vitality, the 'life and rhythm' of people, the visual emphasis on architectural homogeneity, and in fact orthogonal uniformity, is noteworthy (see Fig. 1.2). The rhetoric in this 1962 competition set the agenda for the next half-century, an agenda which persists today, if one considers the goal of enriching the environment, and emphasising openness, attractiveness (including commercial attractiveness) and human vitality.[15]

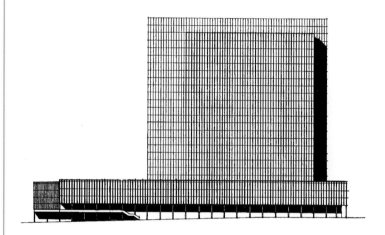

Figure 1.2 Karl Johan-kvartalet, competition drawings, motto 13831, by Håkon Mjelva, elevation, published in *Norske arkitektkonkurranser* No 93, 1963

Orthogonal projections today are in principle the same. Machine lines and shadings have replaced the personal pencil touch, and feature greater care for the outdoor area and context, embellishing the drawings with luxuriant greenery and sometimes people in plans and sections. A recent example of this is shown in the limited plan and design competition for the New Government Quarter in Oslo, submitted in May 2017, which is based on the zoning competition for the same area in 2015. Compared to the typical 1960s and 1970s drawings, the structural system (modules, etc) is no longer underlined, but the distribution of spaces is clearly readable, both inside the buildings and outdoors. The latter is definitely more worked out than 50 years ago, and is emphasised rhetorically with colours for different vegetation, water, and tables and chairs (see Fig. 1.3).[16]

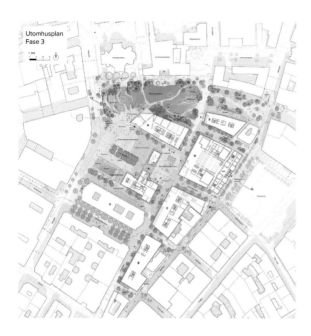

Figure 1.3 New Government Quarter, motto ADAPT, outdoor plan, Statsbygg, 2017

Perspectives — lifelike and seductive

Perspectives bring a visualisation of the building to the immediate perception of the observer within the recognisable context of the site, without necessitating the spatial thinking required by the abstract orthogonal representation of an idea. The use of perspectives has been highly controversial in the history of architectural competitions, and was intensely debated in the 19th century, such as in Britain when RIBA was preparing the 1880 competition regulations. Perspectives and sketches flourished from the Romantic period onwards, and their popularity grew vastly with the explosion of competitions in the 19th century. It was argued that the perspective gave the most 'truthful' image of the prefigured building. In France, perspectives had long been forbidden at the École des Beaux-Arts as 'they were considered falsifying and non-essential representations of the architectural concept'.[17]

Owing to their intrinsic 'realistic' suggestiveness, perspectives can be alluring and treacherous, and the attitudes of architects towards this technique remained ambivalent. In the 20th century, perspective drawings were often replaced by model photographs, which lent weight to the more factual and professional mediation of spatial and structural relations.

Today, computer renderings have taken over the role of hand-drawn perspectives, and have expanded their use and effect dramatically.[18] Combined with photographic representations of the surroundings, computer renderings intensify the realism of appearance and invite the audience to identify immediately with the project as it is proposed. The lifelike character of the visualisation makes the audience, especially the lay person, believe that what they are seeing is the real building, whereas it is in fact a lifelike sketch, a provisional image of something that has to be adjusted, and worked out further. In the example from the limited competition for Kistefossdammen Kindergarten in 2015, which was won by the Danish architects Christensen & Co, the renderings of the exterior show an image which is *almost* credible: children playing outdoors dressed for a rainy day are colourful, but would the wide doors to the interior be open on such a chilly day (see Fig. 1.4)?[19]

Computer-based renderings are effective rhetorical tools. They enable fantastic visualisations of ideas and projects for possible future built environments, in tune with the visual culture which is prevalent today. The competition secretary of the National Association of Norwegian Architects (NAL) is critical of the extent of use of computer renderings in competitions, since they move the focus from the architectural totality to the outer appearance: 'It is important that the jury studies the competition material in depth, and not be deceived by fancy renderings.'[20]

Figure 1.4 Kistefossdammen Kindergarten, by Christensen & Co Architects, perspective playground, 2015

Openness, attractiveness and security

In the limited, parallel commission for the *zoning* of the New Government Quarter in Oslo, in 2015, computer renderings occupied a large space, both on the plates, and in this case, within the very comprehensive A3 reports. The total programmed building space was 115,000 square metres, a huge volume on this central site surrounded by historic buildings. Moreover, as a consequence of the 2011 terrorist bombing, the issue of security was stressed in the brief.

In each of the seven proposals, great emphasis was put on the outdoor spaces and people strolling about the area. The competition material, at all stages, emphasised that 'inviting and attractive openness' should be a central quality.[21] An architecture critic in the newspaper *Dagbladet* featured a two-page presentation pointing out (finally) the contradiction between the 'inviting openness' that was promised and the constraints that are preconditioned by the security and the very function of the area – housing offices for the government. Open access for pedestrians and cyclists in the green and park-like outdoor spaces is not enough: the critic wants shops and coffee shops and restaurants (that are all impossible for reasons of security), and claims that 'good urban development is more important than a padded, totally secured bureaucracy'. 'Government employees in sunset offices,' he remarks ironically.[22]

This touches upon a challenge of contemporary architecture rhetoric, which addresses the emotions of the audience: the obsession with openness and attractiveness. Nobody wants the opposite: 'closed and unattractive'. However, when 'attractiveness' equals commercialism, the rhetoric takes for granted that we, the audience, are totally permeated and conditioned by market liberalism; unable to enjoy environmental qualities that do not equate us to commercial consumers, and neglecting aesthetic pleasures that are available in tranquillity, in uncommercial buildings and in nature.

This last point seems to be accommodated by the 2017 competition for the New Government Quarter buildings in 2017. The ideal of 'inviting and attractive openness' is followed up rhetorically in the texts and visual material, but coffee shops or other shops for the general public are absent. 'Inviting openness' can be partially substituted by 'transparency' – large glass walls that enable visual contact between the public outdoor spaces and the office spaces inside. Large perspective renderings dominate the plates, showing pedestrians and cyclists between the buildings, surrounded by greenery (see Fig. 1.5).

As a result of the 2015 zoning competition, the programmed spaces were considerably reduced. The new zoning, however, permits a four-storey-high extension on top of the central 1958 high-rise building, and thus allows Høyblokka to remain the tallest and most dominant edifice, a decision of symbolic significance since it will continue to house the prime minister's offices.

Figure 1.5 New Government Quarter, motto ADAPT, perspective Grubbegata, Statsbygg, 2017

The challenge of quality assurance and populism

The pretence of transparency, openness and attractiveness, and even mass consumerism, is blurring the invisible power relations and the relentless, gross exploitation of sites typical of contemporary urban areas. Behind the surface of the colourful renderings, many competitions today, and especially those organised by the Norwegian Directorate of Public Construction and Property, Statsbygg, require a huge amount of professional work implying explanations on numerous technical aspects under the umbrella of so-called 'quality assurance'.

Along with the drawings, the (often illustrated) texts are important as rhetoric providing information (*logos*) and credibility (*ethos*) for the competition proposal. Thus, the A3 report of Snøhetta in the parallel commission for the zoning of the New Government Quarter in 2015 was 191 pages long. Moreover, Building Information Modelling (BIM) is now demanded in several competitions. The quality assurance aspect is not only intended for the competition organiser, but cost and safety are also significant issues for the democratic institutions and the general public, who are concerned with 'taxpayers' money'. The space for experimentation is likely to suffer from this situation in contemporary competitions. Moreover, the rhetorical risk is that the total material becomes too comprehensive and impenetrable, since simplification is also a core ideal in both textual and visual rhetoric.

A goal of classical rhetoric is to speak in such a way that professionals think is good, and non-professionals think is true. Competitions still enjoy a high status within the profession, but the autonomy of the field has become more relative, ie dependent on the non-elite influence in society and the media representing the mass culture typical of modern democracies.[23] Competition rhetoric must be prepared to meet increased aggressiveness and critique of the elites, and at the same time not compromise the factuality and credibility that sustain architectural quality.

Notes

1 Christine Smith, *Architecture in the Culture of Early Humanism: Ethics, Aesthetics, and Eloquence, 1400–1470* (Oxford: Oxford University Press, 1992), 82.

2 The use of videos was highly recommended by Marco Brizzi in his talk on communicating architecture at the Norwegian Centre for Design and Architecture, 19 October 2016, in which he stressed the importance of 'moving the emotions' of the audience.

3 Ole Gustavsen, interviewed by Elisabeth Tostrup, 2016.

4 Hélène Lipstadt, 'Experimenting with The Experimental Tradition, 1989–2009: On Competitions and Architecture Research', in *The Architectural Competition: Research Inquiries and Experiences*, eds Magnus Rönn et al. (Stockholm: Axl Books, 2010), 36–75, 63.

5 Barry Bergdoll, 'Competing in the Academy and the Marketplace: European Architecture Competitions, 1401–1927', in *The Experimental Tradition: Essays on Competitions in Architecture*, ed. Hélène Lipstadt (New York: Princeton Architectural Press, 1989), 21–51.

6 Reiulf Ramstad in his talk at the Literary 'Mini Salon', 11 September 2016. Other professionals, antiquarians, engineers and representatives of the users are not trained in interpreting architectural figurations.

7 See Hélène Lipstadt, 'Architecture and its Image: Notes Towards the Definition of Architectural Publication', in *Architectural Design*, No 3/4, 1989, 13.

8 See also Antigoni Katsakou, 'Representation of "Potential Realities" and Contemporary Domestic Myths', in *Space and Place: Diversity in Reality, Imagination and Representation*, eds Brooke L Rogers and Anna Sugiyama (Oxford: InterDisiplinary Press, 2013), 29–40.

9 See Elisabeth Tostrup, *Architecture and Rhetoric: Text and Design in Architectural Competitions, Oslo 1939–97* (London: Andreas Papadakis, 1999), 29–32.

10 Brizzi also pointed out that communication of architecture today is much more concerned with the use of spaces than the object itself (Brizzi, 2016).

11 See also Nicholas Mirzoeff, 'What is Visual Culture?', in *The Visual Culture Reader*, ed. Nicholas Mirzoeff (London; Routledge, 1998).

12 Tostrup, *Architecture and Rhetoric*, 25.

13 Recalling the 1960s in Britain, Peter Smithson said: 'The "package" pre-fabricated buildings at that time, in the 60s, were regarded as being invisible from the outside. The normal procedure was: an architect from the municipality would be approached by a company. They would agree about where to put the building. Nothing else. It was absolutely without control. [...] The municipal architect's committee wasn't interested in what the buildings looked like. They were like supermarkets now, ethically and aesthetically invisible. Nobody was concerned, not even the architects.' Peter Smithson, interviewed by Elisabeth Tostrup, Urbino, 1991. See also *Architecture and Rhetoric*, 162–163.

14 *Karl Johan-kvartalet* was intended to house a theatre, cinema, shops and offices. Here is shown one of the two shared prize projects, the one that was selected for commission, by Håkon Mjelva. *Norske arkitektkonkurranser* (*NAK*), No 93, 1963.

15 In the case of the *Karl Johan-kvartalet* competition, the project was finally turned down after harsh protests against the high-rise which was part of the project, and because people opposed demolishing the existing buildings, especially the facades, facing the main street.

16 http://www.statsbygg.no/Nytt-fra-Statsbygg/ Nyheter/2017/Slik-kan-Regjeringskvartalet-bli/.

17 Bergdoll, 'Competing in the Academy and the Marketplace' in *The Experimental Tradition*, 43.

18 Significantly, computer tools also enable engineering calculations and building industry production methods that were unknown (and not possible) some decades ago, and which enable a vast variety of architectural forms and structures.

19 *Norske arkitektkonkurranser* (*NAK*), No 454, 2015.

20 Per Rygh, interviewed by Elisabeth Tostrup, 2016. He praised an exceptional case, the competition for the new National Museum in Oslo in 2010, where the submitted material of the winner, German architects Kleihues + Schuwerk, was 'bone dry', and did not display a single perspective. The 'perspectives' that were published were model photographs.

21 Statsbygg, *Program for paralleloppdrag. Nytt regjeringskvartal* (Oslo: Statsbygg, 2014). http://www.statsbygg.no/files/prosjekter/RKVnytt/ parallelloppdragene/RKVenglishTranslation.pdf, edited Oslo, 2014. Statsbygg, *Paralleloppdrag. Nytt regjeringskvartal. Evalueringskomiteens rapport*, edited Oslo, 2015.

22 Mikael Godø, '*På den sikre sida* (On the safe side)', *Dagbladet*, 5 December 2016, section Signaler, 32–33. This was published at a point when the zoning plan was about to be passed, and the seven pre-qualified design teams would receive the formal invitation to the plan and design competition.

23 For further reading on populism in architecture, see Hélène Lipstadt, 'Are Competitions Populist? A Bourdieusian Alternative Perspective', in *What People Want: Populism in Architecture and Design*, eds Michael Shamiyeh, DOM Research Laboratory (Basel: Birkhäuser, 2005), and Alexander C Tzonis and Liane Lefaivre, 'In the Name of the People', in *What People Want: Populism in Architecture and Design*.

CHAPTER 3

INTERNATIONAL COMPETITIONS AFTER THE SECOND WORLD WAR (1948–1975) AND THE INTERNATIONAL UNION OF ARCHITECTS

Aymone Nicolas

Establishing trust within the members of the profession

The first decades in the life of the International Union of Architects (UIA) were marked by post-war reconstruction and economic growth in Europe, decolonisation in Africa and Asia, and the Cold War.[1] In retrospect, competition practice seems to have been resilient, despite constant criticisms. European architects, the founders of the UIA, could have defied competition practice because of its links to the eclectic styles of the end of the 19th century, and the monumental architecture promoted by German and Italian dictators. But one of the UIA's first projects was, in fact, to adopt international regulations for competitions to establish trust and facilitate architects competing internationally.

The UIA is a not-for-profit organisation, founded in Lausanne in 1948 by Sir Patrick Abercrombie, Auguste Perret, Helena Syrkus, Paul Vischer, Jean Tschumi and others. The French architect Pierre Vago (1910–2002), UIA's first general secretary, played a very important role in shaping the organisation's practices up until 1969. In the 1930s, Vago was a journalist for the magazine

Figure 1.6 First executive committee of the UIA, Lausanne, 1948. In the foreground Jean Tschumi, Auguste Perret. Fonds Jean-Pierre Vouga, Archives de la Construction Moderne–EPFL

L'Architecture d'Aujourd'hui. In his view, competitions were a response to the building crisis, an opportunity for the Modernists, and a form of state expression. After 1945, Vago applied his universalist ideals and diplomatic skills in his work as UIA secretary and regular jury member. His work mainly involved protecting the rights of participants: equality in the competition rules, reasonable deadlines, copyright and the value of prize awards.

The UIA's archives make reference to 150 competitions, organised in 80 countries over the period, half of which led to commissions. The archives are largely made up of the correspondence between Pierre Vago and the competitions' organisers. Their study confirms that the international competition guidelines, which were first laid out in 1908 by the members of the Permanent International Committee of Architects (CPIA), and finally adopted by UNESCO member countries in 1956, did not encourage experimentation in terms of procedures. At that time, there were two main types of competitions: open or restricted, involving either one or two stages. Open anonymous competitions were preferred as a result of the development of international opportunities. This competition model, 'modern and universal', was gradually called into question in the late 1960s as practices changed.

In its attempt to establish competition rules, the UIA initially focused on the regulation and protection of the profession of independent architects in order to establish trust between the different parties, as the international competition for the Palace of Addis Ababa in 1950 shows. This competition was first launched in 1948 following Emperor Haile Selassie's return to power. Ethiopia was no longer annexed by Mussolini, and had been split between Italy, France and the United Kingdom. The competition was organised by an American and a French consultant. Pierre Vago suggested two external jurors,

Sir Patrick Abercrombie and Jean Tschumi, president and vice-president of the UIA respectively; they were in fact appointed as experts to prepare the groundwork for the Ethiopian jury. Three prizes and four honorary mentions were awarded. The jury recommended a second competition that should be better organised, but the government went ahead and commissioned the winners, Hugo Brunner and Herman Kiers, to construct the palace. Ten years later, the French architect, Henri Chomette, wrote to Pierre Vago about two other Ethiopian competitions, which provided no guarantees to the architects: 'I told you about our attempts to limit the chaos that plagues our professional activities here, what with the various so-called technicians who have vague professions, anything from business agents to contractors. [...] The same applies to all *underdeveloped* countries, where there is still no stable structure for dealing with construction problems.'[2]

From the 1950s to the 1970s, the competition practice was exported to the five continents. This probably improved the status of independent professional architects, who were considered a cultural asset rather than a commercial asset. After 1970, more countries opened up to international selection, for example, Brazil, Iran and Japan. Thus, the UIA organised its action on a regional basis. The UIA gradually engendered in the architects more confidence in themselves and trust in the procedures by encouraging them to apply to international competitions. It also recommended that competition organisers include candidates from overseas or UIA representatives as jury members. Most importantly, the UIA put pressure on organisers to make sure that the winner was given the commission.

Competitions: a discursive tool in the service of international stakeholders

At the time, the majority of large competitions were organised by governments or urban agglomerations, for example, the Kingdom of Ethiopia, the Federal Republic of Germany, the City of Sydney, the City of Toronto, the Persian government. Therefore, the corresponding building types or plans were quite standard: parliaments, opera houses, universities, city halls, central bank headquarters, development or reconstruction plans. Competition titles changed after the 1970s, with the shift of interest towards the renovation of urban centres or mixed-use buildings (congress halls, cultural centres). It should be noted that competitions rarely concerned housing or building projects, such as airports, train stations, nuclear power stations, tourist complexes, ski resorts, radio and television studios, as was typical of the

1960s. Projects of this type were considered industrial innovations; therefore, they were generally designed by engineers, not by architects.

In parallel, numerous international organisations were set up along the lines of the United Nations, and international commissions emerged. Several competitions demonstrate this development, as in the eight European Coal and Steel Communities (ECSC) competitions, organised during the Ghent Fair on the theme of housing European workers,[3] or the competitions for the Auschwitz memorial in Poland, and the Dachau memorial in Germany. In both these latter cases, the organisers' committees were made up of deportees from different countries who wanted to erect a monument to embody the collective memory. This fully justified an international competition calling on artists from diverse backgrounds.[4]

In 1949, the World Health Organization (WHO) launched a restricted competition to build their social headquarters in Geneva, with the help of the UIA. In this case, as with the Dachau and Auschwitz projects, an international competition was used to provide legitimacy to collective commissions. By encouraging dialogue, a more horizontal approach was introduced in a society that still operated under a very hierarchical structure. In competitions during the 1950s and 1960s, dialogue was limited to the jury's sessions. Nowadays, dialogue involves the user, as well as the interaction between the candidates and the jury. Dialogue is essential for all experimental procedures, including the phases of project implementation and construction.

Going back to the WHO competition, the analysis of the UIA archives reveals a costly competition and a brief with heavy requirements, thus raising several questions: Why did the WHO organise a one-stage competition, restricted to 15 invited teams of famous architects, when they could have opted for no competition at all, or else, after eight years of planning, for a competition in two stages? Why did they appoint a prestigious jury, including Sven Markelius, Gio Ponti, Sir Howard Robertson, Pierre Vago, the president of the WHO Executive Committee and the councillor of the Geneva canton? There are two valid hypotheses. The first is that the organiser may have wanted the competition to be seen as a collective decision-making process, and therefore as one that should not be questioned. The second hypothesis is that the organiser sought to erase the effects of the scandal surrounding the competition for the League of Nations Headquarters in 1927, which was an architectural fiasco involving endless diplomatic discussion.

Two particulars of the competition procedure show that the WHO competition was very well organised, and that the building site was well managed. First, André Valot, the public official responsible for planning, visited the headquarters of all the international organisations (for example, the UN, UNESCO, NATO and the World Council of Churches) before and after the competition. On his first trip, he met Jean Tschumi, the architect who actually won the competition, who accompanied him on the second trip. Second, the jury met twice and visited the site. Its report included a comparative assessment, in accordance with the brief, which was quite unusual at the time. The president of the World Health Organization gave the following concluding statement: 'Finally, this project was chosen on condition that the building is lower and more spread out. As the only doctor among the jury's architects, I have found over time that an architectural diagnosis is as difficult as a medical one. Several years on, seeing vertical lines emerging here close by, I know that in architecture, as in medicine, today's truth is not tomorrow's truth.'[5] This statement shows that there was quality interaction among the jury members, and between the commissioners and the architects. This is manifest in the outcome – which is an elegant, modern, rational office building.

Figure 1.7 Jean Tschumi, WHO competition. First prize, site plan, 1960, WHO Archives

Political vision for the emergence of truly innovative architectural styles

To conclude, one can look at another emblematic competition, namely the *Plateau Beaubourg*, or Pompidou Centre in Paris. This competition may be considered emblematic, not only because of its significant impact on French architectural policies of the 1980s and 1990s, but also because of the building that was developed as a result. The competition was launched in 1970, and marks a turning point in the processual framework of international competitions. There was a shift from strictly competitive 'modern and universal' competitions, with basic programmes and assessment criteria, to more diverse competition procedures. This development occurred in response to the need for rationalisation, transparency and dialogue. Developments include the use of quantified assessment (with the help of the first computers), operational planning and user participation (both in the planning and evaluation stages), as well as discussion forums. This example demonstrates the importance of the brief. It also demonstrates the contemporary political vision for the emergence of truly innovative architectural styles.

The idea of a national centre for the arts, design and music was discussed six months after the presidential elections in June 1969. The elections were triggered by the tumultuous civil unrest of May of the previous year, and General de Gaulle's resignation. The launch of an international competition was very unusual for the French government. France had not officially organised any international competitions since the 1930s. The brief was nonetheless extremely innovative, inspired by the systemic analysis of architecture, initiated by Christopher Alexander in the United States.

Georges Pompidou, the French president, instructed the Ministry of Cultural Affairs to organise a one-stage competition of ideas. The aim was typical; namely, to appoint the architect who would be entrusted to execute the project, the French government reserving the right to contract the winner to do a supplementary study.[6] The government worked with a planning commission made up of six senior officials, including the young architect and engineer François Lombard, who had just graduated from Berkeley University with Christopher Alexander, and who later became the UIA competition representative.

Figure 1.8 Georges Pompidou Centre, Renzo Piano and Richard Rogers, Paris, 1977, SIAF/CAPA, Centre d'archives d'architecture du XXe siècle, fonds Georges Candilis

The idea of versatile structures was already in the air, which is why the principles of flexibility, permeability and openness were the keywords of the competition brief. It was also probably the first time that the brief mentioned the users and their 'desires', as well as the notion of 'non-constraining' programming principles.[7] The UIA helped choose the jury, which was chaired by Jean Prouvé and included four museum curators, three architects (Emile Aillaud, Philip Johnson and Oscar Niemeyer) and Gaëtan Picon, professor of humanities and a close friend of André Malraux.[8] The first prize was awarded to the team comprising Renzo Piano, Gianfranco Franchini and Richard Rogers, supported by the engineers Ove Arup and Partners. Experimentation was not only part of the brief, it was central to the jury's criteria: 'In the same spirit, the jury meeting in Paris, in March 1971, to assess 682 projects from 54 countries, prioritised freedom of expression ... no preconceived ideas, no preferences of style or school.'[9] The historian Bernard Marrey also points out that other factors besides its innovative character influenced the building's success – the judges' liberal approach and respect for the rules of the game: 'after preparing the competition brief, the commissioner oversaw the project's execution and, thus, acted as mediator between the future users' desires, the architects' aspirations and the financial reality [...].'[10] The Beaubourg competition served as a reference for reforming architectural policies in France over the next 20 years, which included the organisation of big international competitions (for example, the Grand Arch in La Défense, the Bastille Opera House and the Villette Park).

Three essential qualities emerge from this competition that promote different kinds of experimentation, namely: trust, dialogue and a clear political vision in relation to methodological, social, aesthetic and political aspects of architecture. In particular regarding:

- *Trust:* on one hand, the French government demonstrated their trust in a competitive procedure; in in a new planning approach from the United States; in a controversial team of French and international jurors; and in the winners, despite their youth and foreign nationality. On the other hand, the participants (682 in total, including 190 from France and 150 from the United States) trusted the organisers and the jury.

- *Dialogue:* there were discussions with future users (staff from the museum, the library and the centre of industrial creation), UIA representatives, the jury, and in particular with the winning team. In fact, the government explicitly made a commitment to continue the discussions after the competition phase.

- *Clarity of political vision:* a central point of this competition, and evident in the choice of the site (in the heart of Paris), the nature of the brief, the emphasis placed on ideas (organised in one stage, open to all, anonymous and international), and respect for users' requirements.

In parallel to changing social requirements, the end of the 1960s marked a shift in the UIA's position in terms of developing a dialogue and interpreting a clear political vision in the framework of a specific brief. It was only after the events of May 1968 in Europe that criticism was raised about the competitive system and the juries. For example, the terms 'competition' and 'jury' were replaced by 'consultation' and 'panel of experts' in Monaco in 1969[11]; users were involved as members of the jury and as candidates when the West Berlin council wanted to renovate the Kreuzberg district in the two-stage competition *Strategien für Kreuzberg* (Strategies for Kreuzberg) in 1977.[12] The magazine *L'Architecture d'Aujourd'hui* and the French Union of Architects launched an international consultancy for the Les Halles district as a protest ten years after the demolition of the Baltard Pavilions. From the organisers' point of view: 'six hundred teams demonstrated their belief in architecture, knowing that there would be no material gain. This [...] transforms the consultation into innovation.'[13] In 1978, the UIA regulations took into account the policy changes. They established a third category of 'specific' competitions, namely, the joint competitions of architects and developers, or portfolio-based competitions. These became popular in the 1980s and 1990s. The financial criteria were increasingly important.

At the same time, François Lombard, the UIA competition delegate, encouraged the UIA to study the quality of the brief and ensure that the goals of a competition matched the competition type before it was approved. This was the most significant change at the time, particularly in terms of innovation. In the 1950s and 1960s, competition briefs failed to take account of the users' analysis, needs and interactions. Little attention was given to the financial aspects of the building, or its construction and maintenance costs.

Since then, competition briefs have become more precise, both in terms of the requirements of the building programme and the financial aspect of the projects. At a time when the 40th anniversary of the Beaubourg is celebrated, and its architecture is still perceived as innovative, the question now is: Have financial considerations taken precedence over the political vision of architecture?

Notes

1 Nicolas Aymone, *L'apogée des concours d'architecture, L'action de l'UIA 1948–1975* (Paris: Picard, 2007), 220.

2 Letter from Henri Chomette to Pierre Vago, Paris, UIA archives, box 1/11, dated 1 May 1961 and 12 June 1961.

3 Jury report, *Concours de l'unité d'habitation à l'échelle industrielle*, Revue UIA, No 47, 1967, 26–32.

4 James E Young, *The Art of Memory: Holocaust Memorials in History* (Munich: Prestel Verlag, 1990). Kathrin Hoffmann-Curtius, 'Memorials for the Dachau Concentration Camp', *Oxford Art Journal*, Vol 21, No 2, 1998, 21–44.

5 Inauguration file, Geneva, WHO Archives, A 3-416-3 HQ (E) 1-2.

6 Documents of the brief: *Le centre Beaubourg*, Paris, 1971, 15.

7 Letter from the president to Edmond Michelet, dated December 1969, A.N. CACAP/10. As cited by Eric Langereau in *L'État et l'architecture. 1958–1981. Une politique publique?* (Paris: Picard, 2001), 272.

8 Malraux, minister of culture of the De Gaulle government, who quit politics after 1969.

9 Jury report, *Le centre Beaubourg*, 1971, 21.

10 Bernard Marrey, '*Le centre Beaubourg et la renaissance du programme*', in *Les bâtisseurs de la modernité (1940–1975)* (Paris: AMO/*Le moniteur*, 2000), 201.

11 *Consultation pour un palais des arts à Monaco*, 1969. Fonds Pierre Vago, archives de l'Institut français d'architecture/AN: PP/10, box 215/1, 215/2, 508/.

12 Heidede Becker, *Stadtbaukultur, Modelle workshops, wettbewerbe, 1945–1995* (Berlin: DIFU, Verlag W Kohlhammer/Gemeindeverlag, 2002), 493–501.

13 'Consultation internationale sur le quartier des Halles à Paris', in *L'Architecture d'Aujourd'hui*, No 208, 1980, 1–40.

CHAPTER 4

COMPETITION PRACTICES IN THE UK AND THE ROLE OF RIBA

Discussion with Paul Crosby

Question (Q): For a good number of years you were part of established architecture offices [David Chipperfield, Zaha Hadid] in the UK. Can you give us a glimpse of your experience of architecture competitions, especially in your role as a director of competitions at David Chipperfield's office?

Paul Crosby (PC): I was a director at David Chipperfield's office (DCA) for nearly ten years, subsequently general manager of Zaha's office and then director of Martha Schwartz Partners for a couple of years. During my time in DCA, the majority of our work was won in competition, for a number of reasons. First, because of the economic situation at the time. At the turn of the 21st century there was a recession in the UK. Around the year 2000, there weren't many developers commissioning buildings, and there weren't many cultural projects as the

National Lottery hadn't been set up to fund arts projects; actually, the history of competitions in the UK wasn't particularly established, probably still isn't established, if the truth be told. The majority of competitions were won in countries such as Italy, Germany, Belgium, Holland and particularly in America, and included those for BBC Scotland, the Figge Art Museum, the Public Library of Des Moines and the Anchorage Museum in Alaska.

Q: What types of competitions did you usually choose to enter in Chipperfield's office?

PC: Those were the usual types of international competitions usually involving a call for an Expression of Interest (EOI), a Request for Qualifications (RFQ) type of document, which includes evidence of qualifications, professional indemnity insurance (PII), resources and project experience. The applications are reviewed and reduced to six or so, and they [the applicants] might be asked to attend a briefing meeting, to visit the building or site and then produce a proposal. This might be a sketch proposal or it could be a full design competition.

In DCA, we would never enter an open competition; this was almost an absolute business rule, because it is pot luck. We would go through the criteria of all the competitions and try to understand the chances of winning, and ask whether it presented an interesting architectural opportunity. Also, we preferred that there was a chance to realise a building. We were not particularly interested in the competition remaining on paper, and we always sought to understand how it was going to be funded. Also, importantly, we wanted to understand the judging criteria of the competition, and to know the judging panel. It is important to know how the judgment is made up, and if it is based on fee, design proposal, approach, design team. All that was very important to us, and this is why, particularly in DCA, we were quite successful; the rate of winning competitions was high because we analysed the criteria and gave ourselves an opportunity to explore architecture and win.

American competitions are slightly different from those in Europe as they are more about selecting a team and forming relationships with the client group, and not about the architect doing an excessive amount of work. It was more about doing a sketch, having an idea and then meeting the client team, understanding the brief and talking about an approach and ideas – and how we would go about designing the project. It was more about the *process* rather than the product. I think that competitions in the UK tend to be more about the product, about the building itself rather than the process and relationships. The competition is about choosing a building rather than an architect, and if anything, I would really emphasise the [importance of the] latter; that a good project is the result of the good relationship between a client and the design team. If, in a competition, you do not speak to the client, how can you design a good building; how can you lay it down in terms of a brief represented through plans and sections? The issue is how can you build up that relationship with the client without communication and a briefing process?

Q: Do you think competitions can be platforms for experimentation?

PC: Absolutely, 100% they are.

Q: In building up the relationship with the client you have just described, where or when does experimentation happen?

PC: That is a good question, and the answer is contradictory to what I have just said. If the client is not there at the table when you are designing, you have a certain amount of freedom of interpretation of the brief. At the first stage, when you get to design a project, you are giving your ideas, and that can be exciting because you are not limited to absolutely strict criteria like forms, materials or urban analysis, or whatever the analysis of the project might be. Actually, competitions are an invitation to open up your process a bit more, and to experiment; they are not strict business propositions but experimentations with ideas, and this is a key reason for doing competitions.

Q: In a big and established architecture office, is there a dedicated team working on competitions? Who decides [and how is it decided] who will work on a competition?

PC: Absolutely. In fact, we changed the structure in DCA to manage competitions, the reason being that we had a number of directors running teams, and as all were interested in design, they wanted to do competitions. However, when your studio is structured in a certain way that everybody is building buildings as well as doing competitions, the dynamic of each team can quickly shift if a competition is introduced into a team that is engaged in a technical stage. Competitions and producing construction information are two different operations. A competition requires an instant energy, but

when you [are] building, it is a more even pace. In DCA, we created a competition team, led by a director and made up of designers used to quickly analysing a brief so that they became very practised at responding to a brief, and creating ideas. The team learns how to very quickly understand and analyse the brief, as well as speculating on what the client will respond to. You get into a mode of working. When you are working on construction information or on design details on a Friday, and then on a Saturday you are asked to do a competition, it is a complete mind shift, which is very difficult. I think this was why setting up a competition team was a very good move in DCA. It meant the people who worked on competitions knew why they were in that team and [were] able to work at a very fast pace, since you work on one competition for six weeks and then go into the next one adopting a similar method.

Q: The same people were on the team all the time, or were [they] changing or rotating?

PC: Yes, they were changing, but led by the same director, as he worked very closely with David all the time, bouncing ideas back and forth for each competition. In addition, I think this way of working was effective for David, who is an extremely busy man, working on many different projects at any one time. The pace of a competition is so different that you need an instant response as you go through all that very quickly; the generation of ideas was happening at a very fast pace. We were also interested in people who had the experience to know how to interpret and respond to a brief and a site, and to create ideas, and so it worked, always.

The younger designers sometimes said 'OK, I've been in a competition, I've been in a competition team for six, seven, eight months', and once they got tired – because of the intensity of the competition, which is physically for the body, mentally and emotionally quite exhausting – then they were placed on a project. And in all likelihood, if they won a competition, they joined the team to continue with the design process through to realisation, which for them was very rewarding.

Q: What do you think about the way UK competitions are organised? There is of course RIBA, but also a number of private offices that organise competitions. According to your experience, what are the problems associated with the organisers of competitions in the UK?

PC: I think we are too conservative in the UK; we are too conscious of ensuring that architects entering a competition have experience of that particular building type, or they have an office with a large number of people, or a required turnover, or that they have a particular level of

insurance. All these things should be standard; there should be a standardisation of that sort of data. The essence of the competition should be about the generation of ideas. We in the UK have to ask, why would you do a competition? Wouldn't it be preferable for a client to meet an architect instead and spend time with them, getting to know them and building a relationship? Competitions cost an architect a lot of money; significant sums of money. So much money is wasted on submitting EOIs and/or RFQs. Why don't you (the client) choose at the beginning? So often I hear stories of young studios of 20 or so getting onto a shortlist and being told that they have done a very good design and presentation, and then at the last hurdle the client says 'actually we don't think you can win, you are not experienced enough yet'. Now, I would ask, why does it get to that stage? Decisions should be made at the beginning of the competition as so much time is wasted through decisions like that.

I think another problem with competitions, particularly in the UK, is that there is not enough support in the younger practices, particularly in the case of public projects. Libraries, schools or any type of public community project should be procured via a competition process, and should support young practices. There is no reason why they shouldn't be able to do that. We are just too conservative; there is almost a fear in the UK: you can't be an architect if you are under 50. In Germany, in Spain, in Switzerland, architects are winning competitions in their early 30s. Zaha [Hadid] won the Peak Leisure Park in Hong Kong in 1982, or Foreign Office Architects (FOA) the Yokohama Port Terminal in Japan in 1995 – [there are] so many examples of international competitions won by very young people. In the non-UK competitions, even the established practices have more chances to meet the criteria to enter and win: take David Chipperfield. I wasn't in the office when David won the Neues Museum in Berlin, but he had never built the equivalent of the Neues Museum, and when he won the extension to San Michele Cemetery in Venice, nobody said to him 'How many cemeteries you have done?' The UK is too conservative, and certainly we don't give younger architects the chance to win competitions. Why does one need to have done five libraries to win a library competition? Competitions should be about ideas.

Q: What would be your suggestion [as to] how you would like to see competitions organised within the UK, by whom and why and how?

PC: The system in the UK is hardly ideal, and the process of selecting an architect requires an overhaul. I think it would be good if our institution, RIBA, was at the centre of this, [and] trusted and respected to run competitions. Yes, RIBA has its Competitions Office, but I think RIBA should be at the centre, leading all aspects of the competitions process. It should be a 'natural' decision of all potential clients, developers and institutions to ask RIBA to lead and manage their competition for houses, public projects etc. RIBA should be about excellence; RIBA *is* about excellence. They have an awards system, student prizes and everything else that supports architecture, but in a way an award is always at the end of the process, and here we are talking about the beginning of the process. RIBA has to apply that same energy and bring the excellence of the awards to the competition process.

RIBA should also be thinking about how you select an architect. What is the most appropriate way to select an architect or a design team? Going back to what I said earlier, too often it is about the object – the final proposition instead of the relationship with the architect. I think competitions should start with the idea and be the ultimate result of a strong relationship between client and architect.

Do you know how much architects spend on a competition, in drawings, model-making, printing etc? It can be as much as £45,000–50,000 on a typical competition. As such, for young studios [it] is just impossible to enter competitions, because they simply cannot afford it. I would reduce it to a very simple ideas competition; and do you really need more than six weeks? Maybe not;

just two weeks and an A3 report, and arguably most importantly, a presentation. In my experience at DCA, we didn't really over-deliver: it was a sketch, the essence of the idea, then David would get into the room with the team presenting the thinking behind this idea. Competitions are about the thinking and research as opposed to the rendering of an 'object'. It is too superficial when we see winning entries' images in newspapers or online – but what was the idea behind the drawing?

Q: If one wanted to bring the energy of the award to the competition, this would possibly imply a decision to institute (as with the RIBA annual awards) a competition every year, maybe an ideas competition?

PC: That would be a brilliant idea, absolutely yes. I like the ideas competition, and this should do two things: one, RIBA will get the best results but at the same time support architects, who are currently fighting with costs, to experiment with ideas and their presentations. You don't require a lot of money, a video and five models to convey your project. Why spend all this time, money and energy presenting it? So I think RIBA could run a number of different types of ideas competitions, a student competition, a small-practice one, and on different topics. Established architects wouldn't enter: as I said earlier, they would be interested in entering competitions to build. But

small practices would be interested in doing a competition with the prospect of winning, or having [their proposal] exhibited to show what they could do; how they can present and communicate their ideas.

Q: I understand you would like to see RIBA competitions taking this direction and becoming supportive of competitions that can also help young talented architects in the UK.

PC: Absolutely. To return to something I said earlier, about there being so much energy spent by design teams in competition processes, and somehow turn it around slightly: if architects were more practised about communication, understanding the client's issues to resolve or propose, then competitions could be richer. I think RIBA can really help construct a process whereby the parameters of the project are clear, and architects don't waste their time. The quantity of documents required for a submission is sometimes criminal. RIBA should to be at the centre to help architects be savvy when entering the competition, so they have a chance of winning.

CHAPTER 5

RIBA-USA: A DIFFERENT TAKE ON COMPETITIONS

Discussion with Jonathan Wimpenny, Tim Clark, Angela Brady and Phil Allsopp

Question (Q): In 2016, RIBA-USA celebrated its 20th anniversary. Can you tell us how, and why, it started?

Jonathan Wimpenny, president emeritus RIBA-USA **(JW)**: RIBA-USA was initiated by Tim Clark in Los Angeles and myself in New York in 1996. This was an independent initiative that was later on adopted by RIBA and is now included in RIBA's international chapters. The initial idea was to support British architects working in the United States. At the time, over 600 RIBA architects were present in different US cities, and they formed a very diverse crowd. Their motives for relocating to work in the United States were different and varied. Nevertheless, they all shared a common problem, namely the RIBA reciprocity system (in place since 1972) was suddenly dropped in 1990. As a consequence, RIBA architects had to once again take

all the examinations to become qualified architects in the US.

Frustration and anger was growing, since neither the UK registration body nor RIBA were paying attention to the problem. This is how it all started; it was a grassroots initiative, a conscious decision to do something about the problem instead of just being angry. Educational programmes, conferences, talks and exhibitions promoting British architecture were organised, initially with the support of UK consulates, UKTI (UK Trade and Investment), and partners such as AIA (American Institute of Architects) chapters, the Getty Institute, and individual firms. The events were very popular, and the next step was to create a legal entity: RIBA-USA started as a CHA501C3 charity organisation to receive donations in the US and to be able to fund its activities to promote British architecture in the US. RIBA was involved in the discussions for the formation of the RIBA-USA charity, but there was a lot of confusion until Angela Brady became RIBA president (2011–2013) and drafted a memorandum of understanding. RIBA-USA was initially conceived [as], and continues to be, a network organisation spreading in major American cities, which currently include New York, Philadelphia, Chicago, LA, Phoenix, San Francisco and Washington.

Q: RIBA-USA mentions competitions in its mission statement.[1] Why is that so?

JW: Competitions were mentioned from the beginning in RIBA-USA's statement of priorities, and are now embodied in its charitable constitution and bylaws. It seemed to us that professional architects competing to win projects and secure commissions missed out all other areas pursued among architects, such as the dissemination of ideas, and education and civic engagement. We thought that competitions could be platforms for experimentation in those other areas. The intention was to organise competitions in which architects did not just compete with each other, but instead became interested in the production and dissemination of ideas and engaged in [the] town-planning exercise. For RIBA-USA, which aimed at showcasing British design, architects' participation and education were valued much more

than professional activity for its own sake. Competitions were seen as the vehicle to pursue and enhance what architects do rather than just celebrate architecture projects.

Q: Could you give specific examples of competitions RIBA-USA initiated or was involved in organising?

JW: In 2008, RIBA-USA organised the Miami Dade student competition (My World would be a Better Place If...). I initiated this competition, as president of RIBA-USA, with Phil Allsopp (current president of RIBA-USA), with the full participation of Miami Dade County school board. This participation meant that the students spending time working on their competition entries would receive high school graduating credits.[2] The aim of the competition was to reach out to schools and encourage high school students to use their design skills to comment on their environment. The subject of the competition was intentionally very broad to encompass the various aspects high school students could be interested to explore in their submissions. RIBA-USA prizes were given at the Wolfsonian Foundation in Miami at the annual RIBA-USA conference; one winner went on to receive a scholarship to study architecture at Columbia University in New York. The competition was successful, and achieved its educational aim, but the experiment was not repeated, despite intentions to do otherwise.

Figure 1.9 Mater Academy competition
– first place team

Figure 1.10 Mater Academy competition
– second place team

Figure 1.11 Mater Academy
competition – first prize
certificate

In 2004, RIBA-USA was involved in the DiverseCity Global Snowball international exhibition with a competition to take part in Beijing and Zhengzhou in China. The previous year, Angela Brady (past president of RIBA) had initiated the DiverseCity exhibition, curated by RIBA Architects for Change, to showcase a selection of designs and completed projects by women and Black, Asian and minority ethnic (BAME) architects along with their views and opinions on diversity of people in architecture. The exhibition was snowballing around the world, and we, as RIBA-USA, were involved in discussions with China and installed the current DiverseCity exhibition in China. At that point, the interest in joining the exhibition was so great that a competition was held, and Chinese architects (women and minorities) competed to be included. Out of 300 submissions, we selected 30 projects for the exhibition, which travelled to the venue in the next country on the list.

Q: Could you expand on how the DiverseCity exhibition/ competitions were organised by RIBA-USA, and what were its effects?

Tim Clark, founder and president emeritus of RIBA-USA **(TC)**: The Boston Chapter of RIBA-USA initially brought DiverseCity to the United States. Debbie Bentley was Boston co-chair in the autumn/fall of 2003 and had mailed members locally to call in new material to follow the example of the work initiated at RIBA London by Angela Brady. I was then based in California, and running RIBA-USA, and made contact with Angela to generate work from US architects to go in a similar exhibition at the UK Consulate in Los Angeles.

The idea was to run a US competition of works by women and minority architects based in the US. The work already submitted for Boston would automatically qualify. A panel of judges, that included myself and Angela as well as the deputy consul general, a representative of the Chinese government and the AIA president in LA, assessed the entries in terms of design quality and sustainability. By this time (early 2004), arrangements for the China mission were well advanced, and the Chinese government had agreed to fully fund up to seven participants, among whom would be the winner of the US DiverseCity competition, Annie Chu. With the benefit of official Chinese backing, a new DiverseCity

competition call was then launched for work from women and minorities in China, and to identify and invite two 'minority' architects to come to the United States on a fully hosted reciprocal visit as guests of RIBA-USA in Chicago and Los Angeles... From there on, still under the wing of Angela Brady, the DiverseCity initiative simply snowballed from country to country, gathering new work at each venue. In 2005, a year after the hugely successful RIBA-USA China mission, relations with Chinese partners were flourishing, with visits to RIBA London, New York and Los Angeles. There was also a one-off Chinese delegation visit to Luxembourg, including local tours and an EU-sponsored dinner with local architects, to whom I had promoted Chinese support for DiverseCity during this, the year of Luxembourg's EU presidency.

Figure 1.12 DiverseCity launch speech, Angela Brady

Figure 1.13 DiverseCity Dublin

Angela Brady OBE, past president of RIBA **(AB)**: I saw the need to internationalise RIBA, and to make stronger, lasting links with RIBA-USA via Tim Clark and Jonathan Wimpenny. The DiverseCity exhibition was a perfect way to do this. We had a brilliant team and the Global Snowball was our exhibition of architects with diverse backgrounds, being celebrated around the globe to 34 cities over a six-year period. Our RIBA group, Architects for Change, instigated by Sumita Sinha, was a collection of under-represented groups, including Women in Architecture, which I chaired (2000–2005), the Society of Black Architects, and LGBT architects and disabled architects groups. Together we had a stronger voice, all looking for better recognition and rights within our profession. Rather than be an insular, moaning group, we decided to be a celebratory group and say how fabulous we were, and here were our views and projects – come join us. We were celebrating diversity within our profession, and encouraging others to join us and appreciate us.

The success of the exhibition was everyone's willingness to take part in it; and it didn't cost a lot to bring it around the world. I would literally call someone I knew in a city like Sydney or Auckland and ask if the institute there would be willing to host the exhibition for free and give us ten of their best women in architecture/minority group architects to join the Global Snowball. The exhibition would last for a few days before being packed up again and taken to the next venue. We would help find a sponsor to pay for the return ticket and accommodation if I or one of my colleagues wasn't staying with friends. I would generally give a talk on women in architecture and at the university/society to spread the word. It was a great idea and easy enough to take part in. We even printed the A1 panels in China so they kept their copy in English and Chinese, and they presented us with a hardback A3 book of all the selected shortlist. People were very welcoming all over the world. We followed this up with a website for a few years, which is still there – http://www.women-in-architecture.com Looking back now at what started out as a 'modest' exhibition, it is the most travelled RIBA-backed exhibition, reaching a large global audience at a time when diversity in architecture was much needed, as it still is today; and it was that ease and willingness to collaborate that made it all worthwhile.

Q: It seems RIBA-USA saw the DiverseCity exhibition and competition as a tool to build international relations, a means of architectural diplomacy so to say, and used it to promote architectural exchanges that gave visibility to women and minority groups. In a sense, you seem to have experimented with the architecture competition format and related it to a travelling exhibition which aimed beyond architectural design. Was RIBA-USA ever interested in organising a 'typical' architecture competition?

TC: By the time of RIBA-USA's Annual General Meeting in the summer of 2006, Caroline Davies and myself had formulated a new idea for a competition, again including Chinese participation, but this time global – Building a Sustainable World: Life in the Balance. The competition challenged participants to develop concepts for healthy, vibrant communities, designed to address climate change and reverse, rather than add to, environmental damage. It attracted over 60 entries and had an impressive panel of judges, including Pritzker Prize winner Thom Mayne of Morphosis, and the internationally distinguished Dr Ken Yeang, as well as the then presidents of AIA and RIBA. Autodesk sponsored the competition with secondary support from local manufacturers of solar panels and wind turbines in the LA area. Thanks to additional, very generous, support from RIBA it was possible to fly in 12 finalists and most of the judges to host a live event at the LA A+D Museum to identify the winners and runners-up. A typical certificate for the winning works includes listing all the judges. All the works are stored electronically, including most of the images. First

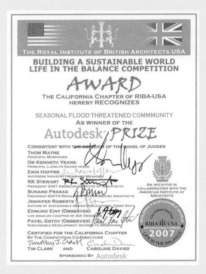

Figure 1.14 RIBA-USA sustainability competition certificate 2007

Prize of $10,000 was awarded to a team from Fiji, Toby Kyle, Chris Cole and Kamineli Vuadreu, for their project, Sustainable Urban Housing in Fiji – Vakabauta Village. However, even in this competition, our main interest and focus was on the social and environmental issues rather than 'flamboyant' architectural design.

Q: What is the current RIBA-USA agenda or approach to competitions?

Phil Allsopp, current president of RIBA-USA **(PA)**: Since taking the helm of RIBA-USA in August 2016, my board colleagues and I – including Tim and Jonathan as past presidents – have been taking a hard look at the core drivers of value that RIBA-USA/ RIBA in the Americas should be

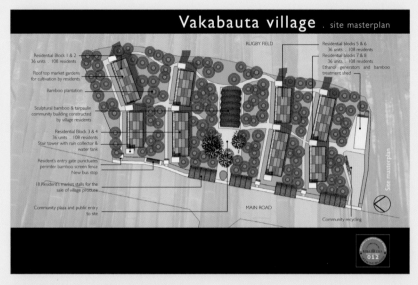

Figure 1.15 RIBA-USA sustainability competition – first prize

delivering to members and society at large, within (and most certainly outside of) the United States. With RIBA's decision to formally recognise an Americas region, it is clear that RIBA will be expanding its activities beyond the United States. Those of us driving RIBA-USA at present already have significant personal and professional relationships in Mexico, and Central and South America, including Colombia, Peru, Brazil and Chile. What's clear is that, in the Americas and beyond, we see a growing and largely unmet need for insights, debates and action on human habitat: the places people live, work, play and learn. We can build on the energy of UN Habitat III, focusing competitions on energising and enlightening future generations of engineers, designers and architects: the children currently in middle schools and high schools. There are a couple of reasons for this: improving the profession's standing and re-igniting creative thinking for future generations.

For all the years of hard work and education, architects are woefully undercompensated and poorly regarded for the enormous value they clearly deliver to clients and to society at large. I therefore harbour a high degree of scepticism over competitions that encourage practising professionals to give away for zero compensation huge value and critical insights to potential public or private sector clients. Architects have for decades been giving away their professional expertise, and the huge economic value that goes along with it, for next to nothing to clients who never consider asking for such low-priced services from physicians, accountants, engineers or attorneys. The consequences for the profession have been uniformly negative, such that architects are too often regarded by business professionals as expensive – and discretionary – blueprint production services. Worse still, perceptions in the business community tend to assume that architects have no real grip on reality or business, and no real knowledge about how buildings get funded and built. This is why 'clients' rep' consultants have had a very easy time of it, moving architects out of the way to limit direct client contact.

There are many ways to overcome the negatives about the profession, but one of them might be through involvement with schools on projects that focus on design thinking and human habitats. A way of showcasing the expertise that architects deliver every day of their careers is to engage them as judges and mentors to up-and-coming generations of future leaders. Architects are very skilled in applying design thinking capabilities to a huge array of social, economic and infrastructure problems. As such, their value to middle and high school students is almost without parallel. There's another reason for getting architects actively engaged in educational technology (K-12) school

projects. There are growing bodies of research that point to the destructive effects on the imagination that 12 years in school can have on incredibly creative children. Given how central creativity and innovation are to being a successful architect, having them part of the schools' competition programme would bring much needed new perspectives to problem-solving, and perhaps rekindle the creative energies that almost every 5–7-year-old brings with them on their first day at school. Re-igniting creative talents will be critical for future generations. They will likely inherit a very different world from our own, and possibly a more dangerous, less accommodating, climate as well.

Q: What are RIBA-USA's future plans for working on competitions with students to address social, human and environmental issues?

PA: In Phoenix, Arizona, RIBA-USA's Phoenix and Southwestern USA Chapter is spearheading an initiative with the City of Phoenix Economic Development Division that will involve high school and community college students attending Hope Academy in reshaping their neighbourhoods to improve their livability in this harsh Sonoran Desert climate. The students come from a wide range of backgrounds, including Native American, Hispanic and Latino communities. Work on this is being scheduled for the fall of 2017.

Q: Did RIBA-USA ever experiment with the format of competitions beyond the confines of architecture?

TC: Organising competitions is a mercurial business that brings magic to the lives of everyone involved. I especially enjoyed the social aspect, and was very humbled by the way people piled in to contribute genuine joy and imagination. In 2006, at the Los Angeles AIA Convention, we ran another competition very much in the spirit of the ones that Phil and Jonathan have been doing around schools with young people. Ours, RIBA-USA Regional and the LA Chapter, was not about architecture this time, but about music and performance. It was with the Verbum Dei High School for disadvantaged children in South Central LA. This school sits in the middle of a very tense Black-Hispanic community with many family, social and drug-related problems, not to mention extremely high criminality and murder rates – there had been a major shooting next to the school the day before I took a visitor from RIBA there.

The kids are therefore survivors in a tough neighbourhood ... They love rap music and would find any excuse to perform it. We gave them such an excuse in the form of a competition to write and perform a rap piece that incorporated keywords such as RIBA, Architect, Buildings, Environment and the names of our sponsors such as

Autodesk and Delta Faucet. You had to be there to believe your ears. We dished out money prizes to these kids on the spot, and thanks to our sponsors we were able to offer a big brunch to all the staff and students who attended. I think Jonathan was with me when the winning singer rapped with the words 'Delta Faucet' ... The sponsor standing next to us was visibly delighted ... But of course, that wasn't the only reason she won. Not quite architecture, but a lot to do with our core concerns about community building, inclusive practices and finding new ways for more diverse groups to have fun and grow together.

We also need at some point to address the difficult issue of who wins and how to lose. This is why we tend to focus on exhibitions; not pass or fail but a place for everyone, bringing people out of themselves onto an open platform away from mobbing, humiliation and isolation. This is a huge prize in its own right.

Notes

1   http://www.architecture.com/RIBA/Working%20 internationally/InternationalNetwork/RIBAUSA/ RIBAUSA.aspx.

2   The school was the Mater Academy Charter Middle/ High School, Hileah Gardens, Miami-Dade County school district.

PART 2

EXPERIMENTING WITHIN
ARCHITECTURAL COMPETITIONS

CHAPTER 6

ARCHITECTURE COMPETITIONS MADE IN DENMARK

Kristian Kreiner

Introduction

This essay describes contemporary forms of architecture competitions in Denmark. Current trends in the design of architecture competitions are analysed, and the great variation between them is illustrated by an extreme case. The picture is multi-faceted, and only a few facets can be discussed here. The facets highlighted are meant to illustrate the variety of approaches, more than give a representative picture.

'Experimentation' is adopted as a frame for the brief discussion of architecture competitions in Denmark. Following a reflection on the meaning of experimentation, the question will be posed whether the observed variety in competition designs qualifies as experimentation.

Trends in architecture competitions in Denmark

The architecture competition is a well-established institution in Denmark. Kim Dirckinck-Holmfeld[1] documents how architecture competitions came to symbolise some of the fundamental values from which Denmark's modern democratic society emerged in the beginning of the 20th century. Such competitions have also played a central role in the development of Danish architecture by giving birth to all major architectural practices, and forming a distinct built environment.

However, the architecture competition is also an institution currently under attack. While being the prescribed manner of public commissioning of architectural services by EU and Danish regulations, it is being criticised for being exceedingly costly and elitist. The criticism reflects a tension between concerns for the creativity, fairness and efficiency of competitions.[2] The open, non-discriminatory competition that seems to maximise the potential for architectural value and continuous rejuvenation of the profession has proven untenable on several counts. First, the total investment in a competition grows rapidly with the number of participants. Also, the burdens on the competition jury grow excessively when having to evaluate and rank numerous entries. Severe time constraints on the jury and the incommensurable qualities of the multiple entries have an impact; the fairness of competitions may also be questioned.

In response to such challenges and criticisms, the restricted (or invited) architecture competition has become the norm. Pre-qualification procedures are designed to select a few architects for the competition, based for example on their prior achievements, specific competencies and financial strength.

Such catering for the concerns of efficiency has increased the focus on the fairness, and creative potential, of competitions. Pre-qualification processes will likely favour large, old and well-known architectural practices at the expense of the young, unestablished and possibly more innovative practices. In response to such concerns, a few young architects have occasionally been invited to the competition as 'wild cards', but this has not silenced criticism of the elitist pre-qualification practice.

When architecture competitions work well, they produce multiple creative design proposals. Design entails not only devising effective solutions to given problems but also original interpretations of these problems.[3] By implication, the competing design proposals are essentially incommensurable, requiring the outcome of the competition to be determined by intractable judgments by the competition jury. The fairness of competitions, and the service to the client's interests, all depend on such judgments. In line with the general trend towards explicit forms of accountability by curtailing the role of (professional) judgments, the openness of the design task to creative interpretation has been limited by increasing *a priori* specification. From competition briefs of merely a few lines,[4] they now encompass several hundred pages and innumerable explicit requirements and restrictions on the design solution. This comes in addition to complex sets of public regulations, for example building codes and zoning restrictions.

It seems as if the design space is increasingly confined. This has at least two predictable effects. First, the design entries become harmonised in compliance with the competition brief, making their ranking more objective and the outcome of the competition easier to justify. Second, however, if the task is thoroughly documented, the rationale of organising a competition to foster new and creative ideas may disappear.

Architects may no longer make sense of the competition as an enactment of their creative and artistic identity, and instead come to see it as a business investment. Such an attitude may explain the criticism of too-low fees and prizes in view of the high costs architects incur from competition briefs demanding more work and deliverables from participants.

The picture drawn here of the development of architecture competitions in Denmark is one of a constant tension (or competition) between different concerns: the concern for eliciting architectural creativity, the concern for the fairness of the competition (both in terms of access to, and the result of, the competitions), and the concern for the efficiency of the competitions (in terms of the costs and burdens put on the participating architects, the jury members and the client). Catering for one of the concerns will expose the other concerns, and will encourage increased attention on these in the next stage. In this sense, the general history of architecture competitions takes on a 'muddling through' character.[5]

In summary, the current practice is one of highly restricted competitions, both in terms of both participation and design space. It is also one of low efficiency, in the sense that the costs to the client and to participating architects are untenably high. Finally, the justification for organising architecture is questioned in view of the design space being repeatedly constricted. Even among practising architects, the general sentiment seems now to be to look for alternative modes of commissioning architectural services.[6] However, in spite of some disenchantment, experimentation with radically new forms of architecture competition is easy to find.

Illustration: the dialogue-based competition

This architecture competition took place in 2008–09, and resulted in a highly acclaimed primary school and public library in a newly settled part of Copenhagen. The competition is thoroughly documented elsewhere,[7] and described in several previous publications.[8] Its hallmark was an extensive ongoing and open dialogue between the competing architects and a group of experts (including members of the jury) hired by the client.

Figure 2.1 Dialogue-based competition for a primary school and public library in Copenhagen, 2008-09, photo of the built project

Dialogues are a common feature of architecture competitions. In their most rudimentary form, question-and-answer sessions are held in the beginning of the procedure to allow the client, for example, to clarify the text of the competition brief, to add or remove rules of the competition, and to further delineate the solution space. These sessions are typically held before the architects set to work. They are meant to prevent architects working on false interpretations of the client's intentions and requirements.

More elaborate forms of dialogue are observed when the competing architects meet individually with the client's experts and representatives. Such meetings allow the client to give feedback on the presented ideas and strategies, to clarify preferences and improve the relevance and quality of the eventual proposals. To protect the legitimacy of the competition, the client must ensure confidentiality to prevent knowledge about ideas and design strategies leaking between competitors.

However, in the present case, such leaking was enforced by design. On several occasions, each architect met with a very large group of experts (including members of the jury) to discuss architectural and engineering design ideas and plans. These meetings had the format of a seminar with the experts not merely reacting to the presentation of the architects but also actively commenting and suggesting ideas and solutions. The competing architects were present at all meetings. They were even encouraged to 'steal' good ideas from their competitors and exploit them in their own designs.

How did such a competition work when, apparently, the most sacred rules of competition were blatantly violated? Some institutional re-engineering was necessary to restore the legitimacy of the competition.

Solving acknowledged problems with new designs

As already suggested, the extension of the written communication in terms of the competition brief is occasioned by the fear of irrelevance and inefficiency. Misunderstandings can be detected in time for them still to be corrected. The client saves the opportunity costs of having only a subset of the invited architects working on relevant design premises. However, confidential feedback to architects on a one-to-one basis threatens the fairness of the competition. Individualised feedback results in a situation where the architects do not compete on the same information. In particular, if jury members are involved, they may offer insights and make suggestions which will be subject to evaluation in the jury.

To facilitate continuous feedback and dialogue without risking the rigging of competitions, all communication took place openly in the co-presence of all contestants. The competition was reformed into the kind of rivalry known from the Renaissance:

> *'[R]ivalry during the Renaissance seems to have contributed to a competitive culture that bred creativity and innovation. To compete, they borrowed from one another, drawing on the techniques and innovations that they most admired from their peers ... With paragone, two equal rivals were compared and celebrated for their relative achievements. Comparing two or more works in this way did not diminish one at the expense of the other.'*[9]

Fragmentation and zero-sum games are not constitutive features of competition. Constantly measuring oneself against what others have achieved, or are doing, creates an impetus to action to match or surpass the best ideas and solutions. The transparency was meant to spur creativity and effort. The implied coopetition[10] was facilitated by promising all competing architects the first prize if they communicated their plans and ideas truthfully and openly.

This design was clearly in conflict with the institutionalised view of legitimate competitions. To make it legally acceptable, a multi-stage procedure was designed. Formally speaking, open dialogues were part of a parallel assignment procedure, and only the final couple of weeks were carried out as a conventional competition. The bulk of the design work was accomplished in the earlier stages, even if a few last-minute changes in the design proposals were observed.

Results and experiences

A highly unconventional competition ended calmly with a unanimous decision. No one challenged the outcome, and the winning design had high architectural value. In this sense, the competition succeeded. However, the success was possibly not a result of the extensive dialogue. Little borrowing of ideas was observed. Generally, the architects worked slower than expected, which was why few ideas existed when they were planned to be shared. By the time ideas crystallised and became shareable, it was too late for competitors to integrate them into their own designs. It was easier to recognise the impact of the feedback from members of the jury. Sometimes the feedback took the form of decrees, resulting in a streamlining of the design proposals.

Conclusion: variety of competitive forms

The constant competition between the concerns for creativity, fairness and efficiency generates unending variety. The general trend towards simplification (in terms of fewer contestants and narrower design spaces) may reflect concerns with commensurability, costs and managerial burdens. However, the increased complexity of the social dynamics, as exemplified above, reflects concerns with quality and relevance. A viable balance between the three concerns has yet to be found in Denmark. In search of such a balance, it is safe to predict that the future of architecture competitions will hold more change and variety.

Variety and experimentation

The observed practices in organising architecture competitions in Denmark could reflect a continuous experimentation with form and procedures. Experimenting is essential to our belief in learning and progress over a period of time. However, experimentation may mean more than just repeated variation. Selection and retention processes are also necessary ingredients in reorganising competitions.[11]

A dictionary definition of experimentation is:

> *'A tentative procedure; a method, system of things, or course of action, adopted in uncertainty whether it will answer the purpose.'*[12]

Accordingly, experimentation is characterised by trying things out; deciding on ways of performing that we do not know will work satisfactorily in view of some purpose. The reference to 'procedure', 'method', 'system' and 'course' suggests that experimentation is not random. Experimentation is a conscious choice. However, the choice is *tentative*, because it is not known whether things will work. If such knowledge already existed, there would be neither need nor justification for experimenting. The tentativeness of the choice does not imply that the decision-maker is ignorant. He or she may have good reason to believe that what they plan to do will answer the purpose. However, experimentation entails that the results are uncertain to a greater or lesser extent, and *finding out is a motivation for the experiment*.

Thus 'experimentation' has a *dual purpose*. Architecture competitions are organised to build buildings, cities and societies. When they are also experiments, they are designed to teach us how the procedural design works in view of the multiple concerns discussed above. The design and the enactment of the competition reflect a trade-off between the instrumental and the learning purposes. The more emphasis that is put on succeeding with the competition, the more difficult it will be to learn from the experience.

Across all the variation in competition procedures, we observe a very high success rate. Even radically unconventional architecture competitions seem to end successfully, both in terms of the quality of the design proposals and the legitimacy of the winner.[13] The enactment of the competition seems consistently to erase any evidence of the effects of the original procedural design. Nobody seems willing to risk failing to learn the relative strengths and weaknesses of the competition designs. Even if such willingness existed, it would be exceedingly difficult to learn anything valid, except that any procedural design will do. Thus there may be little else to do than to continue the muddling through of the past.[14]

Notes

1 Kim Dirckinck-Holmfeld, *Dansk arkitektur – konkurrencer 1907–1968* (Copenhagen: Bogværket, 2016).

2 Kristian Kreiner, 'Paradoxes of Architectural Competition: The Competition between Efficiency, Justice and Creativity', in *Procs 26th Annual ARCOM Conference, 6–8 September 2010*, ed. C Egbu (Leeds: Association of Researchers in Construction Management, 2010), 441–50.

3 Kristian Kreiner, 'Organizational Decision Mechanisms in an Architectural Competition', in *Research in the Sociology of Organizations*, eds Alessandro Lomi and J Richard Harrison, Vol 36, 2012, 399–429.

4 Ross King, *Brunelleschi's Dome: How a Renaissance Genius Reinvented Architecture* (London: Chatto & Windus, 2000), 1.

5 Charles Lindblom, 'The Science of "Muddling Through"', in *Public Administration Review*, Vol 19, No 2, 1959, 79–88.

6 Danish Association of Architectural Firms and the Danish Association of Architects, *Transaktionsomkostninger ved projektkonkurrencer* (Copenhagen: 2016).

7 Kristian Kreiner and Peter Holm Jacobsen, *Dialog og konkurrence: Eksperimenter med nye arkitektkonkurrenceformer* (Copenhagen: Nyt fra Samfundsvidenskaberne, 2013).

8 Kristian Kreiner, 'Balancing Multiple Matters of Concern', in *Conditions*, Vol 7, 2011, 12–17. Kreiner, 'Organizational Decision Mechanisms in an Architectural Competition'. Kristian Kreiner, Peter Holm Jacobsen and DT Jensen, 'Dialogues and the Problems of Knowing: Reinventing the Architectural Competition', *Scandinavian Journal of Management*, Vol 27, No 1, 2011, 160–66.

9 Bernard Ferrari and Jessica Goethals, 'Using Rivalry to Spur Innovation', *McKinsey Quarterly*, May 2010, 5.

10 Paul Chiambaretto and Herve Dumez, 'Toward a Typology of Coopetition: A Multilevel Approach', in *International Studies of Management & Organization*, Vol 46, No 2–3, 2016, 110–129.

11 Karl Weick, *The Social Psychology of Organizing* (Reading, Massachusetts: Addison-Wesley, 1969).

12 Oxford Educational Dictionary Online. http://www.oed.com.esc-web.lib.cbs.dk

13 For another extreme case, see Kristian Kreiner, 'Built-in Innovation and the Ambiguity of Designing Accessibility', in *Construction Innovation*, eds Finn Ørstavik, A Dainty and Carl Abbott (London: Wiley-Blackwell, 2015), 29–45, and Kristian Kreiner, 'The Inaccessibility of Building Accessibility: Giving Visual and Material Form to Innovation', in *Architectural Competitions: As Institution and Process*, eds Magnus Rönn, Gerd Zettersten and Jonas Andersson (Stockholm: The Royal Institute of Technology, and Fjällbacka: Kulturlandskapet, 2016), 35–61. For an exception to the rule of success, see Kristian Kreiner, 'The Competition Between Creativity and Legitimacy', in *Architectural Competition; Project Design and the Building Process*, eds Jan Silberberger and Ignaz Strebel (London: Routledge, 2017), 45-58.

14 Lindblom, 'The Science of "Muddling Through".

CHAPTER 7

EXPERIMENTATION WITHIN SWEDISH COMPETITIONS

Magnus Rönn

In the following short essay, the use of competitions in Sweden, as well as their operational framework and formats, will be discussed; competitions will also be commented upon as a professional laboratory and an experimental arena for the development of innovative solutions.

The essay will be limited to competitions which are cited by Architects Sweden.[1] On its homepage, it is possible to find a) architectural competitions; b) developer competitions; c) Europan[2]; and d) student competitions, all approved by the association, in the sense that their briefs and conditions have been appropriately checked by Architects Sweden. Of special importance for the organisation is the relationship between the submission requirements and the remuneration of competing architects.

Architects Sweden features an office for competition and procurement services that conveys advice to potential competition organisers. The homepage of the organisation also offers support for drawing up programmes, secretaries for juries and competition officials.[3] Seven elected representatives of the organisation form, along with the four people permanently manning the office, a complementary part of it. Their task is to examine and approve the competition briefs; they also appoint the organisation's representatives in the jury – usually two, according to established competition rules.

Architects Sweden and competition culture

Architectural competitions, as presented on the homepage of Architects Sweden, represent a professional culture, and a way for understanding a special practice passed on to students, architects, architectural firms and potential organisers. On its homepage, Architects Sweden highlights many advantages that competitions hold for clients, politicians, the public and the architects. In Sweden, the public sector is a dominant organising body through municipalities, governmental authorities and public real estate companies.

The merits of competitions can be summarised as follows[4]:

- *A value-creating process:* An architectural competition, where the participants invest their creativity and competence to create the best solution for the task, is a value-creating process for the organiser. The competition reveals how the competition site may be enhanced by new values.

- *Development and innovation:* Competitions are an established tool for programming and design which allow space for development and innovation. Competitions give organisers access to alternative solutions for the assignment.

- *Knowledge and education:* Competitions generate knowledge about the future through design. The solutions for design, economy and user needs may be weighed against each other until the jury finds the result which is most suitable for the assignment.

- *Media impact and news value:* Competitions attract attention, which stimulates public opinion and marketing. The news value creates interest among the public, politicians, architects and the press.

- *A cultural event stimulating public debate:* Competitions generate a basis for public dialogue about architecture as a building culture. Exhibiting presentations make the proposals known to citizens, and they can be discussed in a qualified forum.

- *An approved selection procedure and negotiation for architect services:* Competitions are regulated by the Swedish Public Procurement Act and can be used for public building and planning assignments. For public negotiators, competitions are a method of implementing a project supported by the law.

Architects Sweden emphasises so many competition qualities that a counter-question forcibly emerges: If competitions are so full of advantages, why aren't they more numerous? That Architects Sweden avoids the question (while marketing competitions on its homepage) is not surprising, as the issue of young architects not being invited to pre-qualification competitions is a great problem. The shortage of open competitions is another problem. There is also criticism of the exorbitant resources demanded both by organisers and architectural firms for organising a competition. In addition, many competitions and parallel commissions are carried out without any control from Architects Sweden, and with poor terms for the architects. On the homepage the association promotes approved competitions, which means that Architects Sweden has checked the conditions in the brief and found them to be acceptable.

An illustrative example is the developer competitions (and allocation competitions) that started in Sweden as a result of deregulation of the building sector in the 1980s, and which are now far more common than traditional architectural competitions. The deregulation shifted the production of architecture and urban design towards perspectives important for the private sector, constructors and real estate companies. Still, there are no national rules for developer competitions. The municipalities steer this new kind of competition in three ways: 1) politically through local guidelines; 2) professionally through conditions in briefs; and 3) administratively through land allocation agreements with the developers.

The first known research on developer competitions in Sweden is a case study from 1988. In developer competitions, design teams compete entirely at their own expense; the architects' position in these design teams is complicated. Architectural firms are not a part of the land allocation agreement between the municipality and the developers, who get access to a site for the winning project. The fact that only a few developer competitions are arranged in conjunction with Architects Sweden is also demonstrative of the problems encountered in their processual framework, especially with respect to participating architects.

It is also significant that (in 2012) Architects Sweden carried out an inquiry into competitions on the grounds of two critical motions presented at the organisation's annual meeting. A committee was appointed with representatives of architectural firms and clients for architectural services.[5] The author participated as a representative of academic research. It soon became clear that the committee was primarily interested in professional experience from established architects and organisers of competitions in Sweden, not in research findings from international, European or Nordic studies on competitions in architecture and urban design. The competition and procurement units were not ready to go so far as to suggest new regulations based on research in competitions. At this point, the committee emerged as a conservative protector of its own interests.

A view of the current situation

On its homepage, Architects Sweden presented 12 completed competitions in 2015 (see Table 1, below). Three of those are student competitions where submissions oscillated between 17 and 45 in number, and the winner was awarded 20,000 SEK. There are nine completed competitions for established architects on the homepage. Six are invited project competitions organised by the municipalities and public building companies. Only chosen candidates may participate in invited competitions after pre-qualification. Two of the competitions in 2015 were open ideas competitions where the organiser does not promise an assignment to the winner. In these competitions, young architects and newly founded firms can compete with experienced architects.

Table 1: Completed competitions 2015 (homepage Architects Sweden)[6]

Competition type	Competition task	Organising body
Student competition	Cafe in concrete (Theme: new eyes on concrete)	Stockholmmässan/Nordbygg, STD companies, Swedish Concrete + Architects Sweden
Student competition	Cafe at tube station (in ceramics)	Byggkeramikrådet + Architects Sweden
Student competition	How barriers in a city can be overcome by design (all-inclusive)	Oyster 2015 + Architects Sweden
Invited project competition	Culture centre	Falkenberg municipality + Architects Sweden
Invited project competition	Public space at a harbour	Norrtälje municipality + Architects Sweden
Invited project competition	Plan for a housing area	Stockholmshem + Architects Sweden
Invited project competition	Exhibition building	Örebro municipality + Architects Sweden
Invited project competition	University building	Akademiska Hus, Swedish Transport Administration, Gothenburg municipality + Architects Sweden
Invited project competition	Public space in the city	Gävle municipality + Architects Sweden
Open ideas competition	Homelessness (strategies for improving living conditions)	Stockholms Stadsmission and Stockholm City + Architects Sweden and Architects Without Borders
Open ideas competition	New family house in Dalsland	Leader Dalsland Årjäng, municipalities in Mellerud, Dals-Edm Bengtsfors, Vänersborg and Årjäng + Architects Sweden
Europan 14	Theme: productive cities (selection of sites)	General information on how to take part in the competition as organiser

Figure 2.2 Architect and illustration: FOJAB arkitekter (Sweden), first-prize winner (250,000 SEK), school and library in Falkenberg, 2015. Invited project competition including four competing architectural firms

Figure 2.3 Design: Jim Brunnestom, Hampus Berndtson and Magnus Hellum (architectural students, Copenhagen, Denmark), first-prize (200,000 SEK) winners (out of 122 entries) at the 2015 competition for a single-family house in Dalsland

Figure 2.4 Design: MAP (Malin Arkitektur & Projekt, Sweden), first-prize winner (pro-bono) of the open ideas competition for the homeless. The competition generated 37 design proposals. 35 of them fulfilled the demands of the brief and were evaluated by the jury

The 2016 homepage of Architects Sweden shows 16 running or completed competitions (see Table 2, below). Of those, four are student competitions. Twelve competitions are addressed at practising architects. Seven competitions are by invitation: one ideas competition and six invited project competitions. Four open competitions are found on the homepage: two open ideas competitions and two open project competitions.

Table 2: Ongoing and completed competitions 2016 (homepage Architects Sweden)[7]

Competition type	Competition task	Organising body
Student competition	Shelter for all	NCC, KTH, Dome of Visions and Be Urban + Swedish Architects
Student competition	Theme: Koya (wooden house)	Japan Institute of Architects + Swedish Architects
Student competition	Design of market hall and ceramics	Byggkeramikrådet + Swedish Architects
Student competition	Future housing	Willa Nordic + Swedish Architects
Invited project competition	Extension of town house	Uppsala municipality, real estate company + Swedish Architects
Invited project competition	Housing block	Fastighets AB Förvaltaren (real estate company) + Swedish Architects
Invited project competition	Housing area	Linköping municipality, real estate company + Swedish Architects
Invited project competition	Hospital building	Västfastigheter (real estate company), SveaNor Fastigheter (management company) + Swedish Architects
Invited project competition	Design of a memory place	The National Property Board of Sweden and Public Art Agency Sweden + Swedish Architects
Invited project competition	Culture house	Gothenburg municipality and Higab + Swedish Architects
Invited ideas competition	Urban design of a station	Jönköping municipality + Swedish Architects
Open ideas competition	Development of region	Region Skåne + Swedish Architects
Open ideas international competition	Design of a climate facade shell	Örebro municipality + Swedish Architects
Open project competition	Park of the future	Gothenburg municipality, AB Framtiden (real estate company) and 02 Landscape Architects + Swedish Architects
Open project competition	Culture centre and hotel	Skellefteå municipality + Swedish Architects
Invited developer competition	Housing area	Örebro municipality + Swedish Architects

Figure 2.5 Design: Wingårdh Arkitektkontor and BuroHappold (Sweden/Denmark), first-prize winner (out of 22 entries resulting in four pre-qualifications each awarded 500,000 SEK) for the invited ideas competition organised by Jönköping municipality; the competition language was English

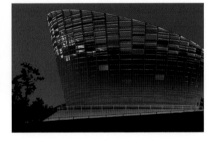

Figure 2.6a and 2.6b
Design: Ett ark (Sweden), first-prize winner (300,000 SEK) of the 2016 open ideas competition for a new climate-shell for the city's water reservoir, municipality of Örebro (60 entries); although the competition was considered an international one, the language of the competition was Swedish

Looking in particular at the developer competition for a new housing area in the municipality of Örebro (featured in Table 2), it is worth noticing that, although it was carried out in cooperation with Architects Sweden, there was no architect of the association appointed to the jury. Nor was there any compensation for the design teams mentioned in the brief. The design teams

Figure 2.7 Design: Slåttö and CF Møller (Sweden/Denmark), winning proposal (out of five pre-qualified participating teams) of the 2016 developer competition for a new housing area by the water in the municipality of Örebro

absorbed all costs for development, while profit was to lie with the developer as a real estate manager gaining access to buildable land. The architects could only hope for a continued assignment. They were not included in the land allocation agreement.

Developer competitions represent a clear shift in power.[8] The public organiser shifts the control over the competition from the city planning office to the real estate department, which in this case plans the competition, controls the land, suggests the jury members and concludes the land allocation agreement with the winner. Similar shifts in power are found in the private sector among consulting, building and property companies. The architectural firms lose the influence of the design team to the developers, constructors and property managers. The architects behind the proposals are invisible in land allocation agreements. Changes occur even in the brief, as for example in the assessment criteria for the proposals. Economy and design are in this case the prioritised values.

The competition world as seen by Architects Sweden

The competition world, as seen through the eyes of Architects Sweden, could be summarised in the following model (see Fig. 2.8), where various types of competitions, regularly organised in Sweden, can be found.

The architectural competition as a key concept includes various kinds of competition procedures that are described on the homepage of Architects Sweden; however, it does not include parallel commissions. An explanation

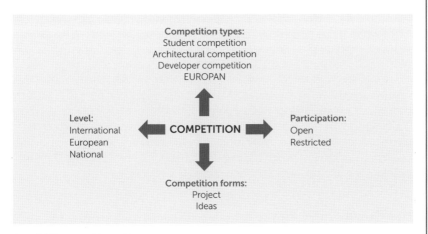

Figure 2.8 The competition world

for the lack of parallel commissions is that these are generally carried out as invited dialogue competitions,[9] without the approval of Architects Sweden. They are not organised according to the competition rules, which demand anonymous presentations of design proposals and conditions approved by the association. Thus, they are not included on the homepage of Architects Sweden.

Apart from student competitions, there are open competitions and restricted competitions, organised as project competitions and ideas competitions. The open competitions are classified as international ones, even if the language in the briefs is Swedish. The design teams participating in invited competitions have an interdisciplinary character, which reflects the complexity of the tasks that contemporary architecture and urban design need to address. Europan is marketed by Architects Sweden as a recurring European competition for young architects.

The architectural competition as a professional laboratory

Architects Sweden promotes the competition as a professional laboratory and an arena for new thinking in architecture and urban design. It is a designer's way of thinking about knowledge.[10] Out of the competition come design proposals expressing architectural values and intentions. Qualities in architecture are embedded in competition, both as a research subject and as a professional laboratory. Architectural quality and intentions in design are to researchers in architecture what measurable characteristics, facts and objective reality are to natural science.

During the competition, innovations in its process framework can appear in at least four different typical documents: 1) the brief; 2) the design proposals; 3) the jury report; and 4) in agreements that regulate the execution of the winning design.

There are also four clearly delimiting stages in competitions, each with their own key players, which steer innovations. In the initial planning, the organising body lays the foundation for new thinking through the choice of jury, competition type and requirements in the brief. At this point innovation might mean changing their own administration by breaking with established routines and trying new suggestions.[11] This kind of procedural innovation can then be incorporated into the brief and shown as a new condition.

A key player in the second phase, responsible for innovation, is the design team. Its task is to find creative design solutions for the assignment. The responsibility is then transferred to the members of the jury who are accountable for judging the proposals and evaluating design solutions. The jury's task is to identify innovative solutions and point out the overall best design in the competition. In the fourth stage, the responsibility returns to the organiser, who as client answers for the implementation of the winning design proposal. The accounts show that innovations in competitions are a collective concern that swings back and forth between the organising body, the design teams, the jury and the client.

The theory of competition as a professional laboratory is derived from the ability to support creativity and new thinking. It is a future-oriented exploration of possibilities; the design teams' proposals present several alternative answers to the competition's question. The organiser acquires knowledge about the future by way of presenting the competition task, inviting design teams and then testing their design solutions.[12] Seen this way, the competition may be described as the archaeology of the future – not as it is, but as it could be found on the site if design proposals were turned into a built environment.

The jury, together with the expert advisers, has a key role in finding innovation in competitions. They must judge proposals and legitimise a winner in a process which has three stages: 1) the design solutions are evaluated first with regard to the criteria in the competition brief; 2) the design proposals are then compared with each other; and finally 3) the design proposal is tested against a 'fictitious reality'. This means that the jury sets out to experience the design solutions as built environments, through the reading of the submitted boards, and the drawings and illustrations produced by the design teams. The ability of the jury members and the expert advisers to see the proposals as architecture depends upon their background, education, professional competence, experience, judgment and involvement.

The theory of competition as a professional laboratory can now be summarised in a number of requirements to be fulfilled. There must be:

- *A description of the competition's purpose (which may contain one or several goals).*

- *A list of criteria for judging the proposal (which can be open and assessable or specific and measurable).*

- *An explanation of the application requirements and competition terms (which the candidates must fulfil).*

- *A group of competent judges (who can be experts in architecture, building design and urban design or representatives of the planned enterprise and politicians).*

- *At least three suggestions from design teams (which can be made up of different professions and companies).*

- *A judging process which evaluates proposals, compares solutions and tests designs according to submission requirements and criteria.*

- *A jury report describing decisions and the motivations behind them in a clear statement.*

The theoretical foundation of the competition as a professional laboratory may be

illustrated by the following conceptual model, which has three levels (see Fig. 2.9).

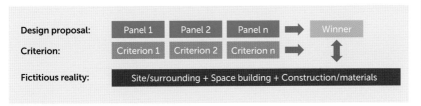

Figure 2.9 Competitions as a professional laboratory

At the first level of the competition, design solutions are presented with panels. The presentation should usually include the context, site, building design and technical system. The panel format differs depending on the task, but follows a specific layout where design proposals are presented by drawings, projections, illustrations, models, diagrams and maps.

Level two of the model should include criteria for assessment. The jury's competence in testing the proposals is closely linked to professional observation.[13] The use of 'soft' criteria for judging values and 'hard' must-have demands for the delivery of design proposals according to the brief is typical for competitions in architecture and urban design in Sweden.[14] The soft criteria have an open character that gives the jury a lot of room for interpretation. The organiser uses the must-have requirements to eliminate candidates lacking the appropriate qualifications.

The criteria in the competition brief specify what the jury should scrutinise: members' attention is directed towards specific aspects of the entries. By questioning the design proposals, the jury acquires responses about how the competition goal might be achieved.[15] A kind of dialogue is initiated which leads the jury to recognise the qualities, defects and uncertainties in the design.[16] Judging is both learning and creating knowledge by interpreting the design in proposals. This can be seen in jury reports as architecture-critical statements. Critique is the foundation for assessments of architectural design.[17]

The third level of the model is called 'fictitious reality'. This means that the competition procedure has an external object hidden in the brief, but which nevertheless influences the jury's understanding of the competition. It may sound strange, but judging is about seeing the proposal as architecture and experiencing the design in three dimensions, as if the site were already built. The jury members put themselves 'inside' the illustrations when they are trying to understand the design. The photographic exactitude of the computer representations enhances the jury's experience of proposals as a built environment.[18] A fictitious reality of alternative solutions is explored.

The point is that the jury compares the design solution in three steps: first with the criteria in the programme, then with each other, and finally with the architectural experience created by the proposed designs as visualised models of the future. The proposals which gain the jury's approval continue to the final step.[19] Here the jury generally sees that one proposal suits the place better than its competitors. The eye will make the final decision. The basic principle in the design solution must be made visible for the jury, and is therefore expressed in illustrations and models rather than in cross-sections and drawings edifying the construction that provide information on how to implement the project.

Conclusion

Three major observations can summarise this essay on the use of competitions in Sweden, their formats and framework.

First, Architects Sweden markets several different kinds of competitions on its homepage, all organised in cooperation with the association. There are competitions for both practising architects and students in interior design architecture, urban design and landscape architecture. Architects Sweden is actively trying to introduce students to the competition culture. The competition is emerging as a very important activity for the organisation. The critical question is whether there are enough competitions organised to maintain an effective culture and develop architecture, creating skilled organisers and providing commissions for architectural offices.

Second, Architects Sweden points out on its homepage that the competition is an area for creativity and new thinking. This is a characteristic that can be applied to the competition as a professional laboratory for the development of innovative solutions. The approved competition has the possibility to fulfil the theoretical demands of being a professional laboratory. The organisation's recommendations stress that the competition is a process that creates space for creativity. Similar criteria reappear in the client's brief for judging the design proposals. According to both Architects Sweden and the competition organisers, the mission for the design teams is to produce innovative solutions.

Third, the organisers responsible for the development of innovations in the competition are invisible, both in recommendations from Architects Sweden and in the competition briefs. They only see design teams as an innovative key actor. However, as the organiser, the client is responsible for the two important stages of the competition process, which can be used for new thinking: pre-competition, when the brief is produced, and post-competition, when the best design proposal is going to be implemented. The client can develop procedural innovation in the brief and has the ability to test innovative ways by ensuring certain qualities in the winning design. None of these possibilities for innovation in architectural competitions can be seen in the homepage of Architects Sweden.

Notes

1   Architects Sweden is the main professional organisation for architects, interior architects, landscape architects and spatial planners in Sweden, with 13,000 members (including 2,600 students). http://www.arkitekt.se/in-english/

2   Europan is a competition for architects under 40 years old, and is conducted every other year by member countries of the European Union.

3   See *Arkitekttävlingar* (Architectural competition), Architects Sweden http://www.arkitekt.se/wp-content/uploads/2014/06/

tavlingsbroschyr2008webb.pdf, and *Parallella uppdrag* (Parallel commission), Architects Sweden: http://www.arkitekt.se/wp-content/uploads/2014/06/Parallella-uppdrag-broschyr.pdf.

4   See: *Tävlingar* (Competitions), Architects Sweden: http://www.arkitekt.se/bransch/tavlingar/.

5   See *Projekt utveckla tävlingsverksamheten* (Develop competition activities), Architects Sweden: http://www.arkitekt.se/projekt-utveckla-tavlingsverksamheten/.

6   See: *Arkitekttävlingar* (Architectural competition), Architects Sweden: http://www.arkitekt.se/wp-content/uploads/2014/06/tavlingsbroschyr2008webb.pdf.

7   Ibid

8   Magnus Rönn, *Prekvalificering – arkitekttävling vs markanvisningstävling* (Stockholm: TRITA-ARKForskningspublikationer, 2012), 3.

9   In a dialogue competition, the client/jury and the design teams discuss the proposals and how the design can be developed. The design teams present their ideas and get feedback from the client/jury before they present the final design solution.

10 Nigel Cross, 'Designerly Ways of Knowing: Design Discipline versus Design Science', *Design Issues*, No 3, 2001.

11 Silvia Forlati, Anne Isopp (eds), *Wonderland Manual for Emerging Architects* (New York: Springer, 2012).

12 See Antigoni Katsakou, 'Collective Housing Competitions in Switzerland. The Parameter of Innovation in Architectural Conception', in *Nordic Journal of Architectural Research*, Vol 21, No 2/3, 2009; *Architectural Competitions: Histories and Practice*, eds Jonas Andersson, Gerd Bloxham Zettersten and Magnus Rönn (Hamburg: Rio Kulturkooperativ and Royal Institute of Technology, 2013); Pedro Guilherme and João Rocha, 'Architectural Competition as Lab: A Study on Souto de Moura's Competition Entries', In Andersson

et al. (eds), *Architectural Competitions: Histories and Practice; Architecture Competitions and the Production of Culture, Quality and Knowledge. An International Inquiry*, eds Jean-Pierre Chupin, Carmela Cucuzzella and Bechara Helal (Montreal: Potential Architecture Books, 2015).

13 Michael Polanyi, *The Tacit Dimension* (New York: Doubleday, 1966).

14 Magnus Rönn, *Prekvalificering – arkitekttävling vs markanvisningstävling* (Stockholm: TRITA-ARKForskningspublikationer, 2012); Magnus Rönn, 'Choosing Architects for Competitions – Reviewers' Experiences from the Selection of Design Teams in Sweden', in *FORMakademisk*, No 1, 2014.

15 Charlotte Svensson, 'Architectural Persuasion: On Quality Assessment in an Architectural Competition', in *Nordic Journal of Architectural Research*, No 1, 2012.

16 Charlotte Svensson, 'Speaking of Architecture. A Study of the Jury's Assessment of an Invited Competition', in *Nordic Journal of Architectural Research*, No 1, 2009.

17 See Wayne Attoe, *Architecture and Critical Imagination* (New York: John Wiley & Sons, 1978); Kathryn Anthony, *Design Juries on Trial: The Renaissance of the Design Studio* (New York: Van Nostrand Reinhold, 1991); Gustav Lymer, *The Work of Critique in Architectural Education* (Gothenburg: University of Gothenburg, Faculty of Education, 2010); Magnus Rönn, 'A Theory for Assessing Quality in Architecture Competitions', in *Nordic Journal of Architectural Research*, No 1, 2012.

18 Antigoni Katsakou, 'The Competing Generation', in Andersson et al. (eds.), *Architectural Competitions: Histories and Practice*.

19 See Rönn, *Prekvalificering*; Svensson, 'Architectural Persuasion'; Leif Östman, 'An Explorative Study on Municipal Developer Competitions in Helsinki', in *FORMakademisk*, No 1, 2014.

CHAPTER 8

MANAGERIAL PRACTICES IN DUTCH COMPETITIONS AND THE IMPACT ON ARCHITECTS

Leentje Volker and Marina Bos-de Vos

Introduction

The Netherlands has often been portrayed as a fertile ground for young architects, giving rise to internationally acclaimed firms such as MVRDV, OMA, Mecanoo and UN Studio. Competitions play a pivotal role in the development of young firms, but are also key to the continuity of established practices. Until recently, Dutch architects experience difficulties in acquiring projects from competitions. The number of construction projects has been limited because of the significant downturn in the Dutch construction market caused by the global financial crisis (2007-08). The number of privately funded commissions also decreased but is slowly starting to grow now. The Dutch government, which initially decided to stimulate the construction industry by speeding up certain investments, limited expenses significantly, resulting in fewer public commissions. Many (semi) private clients have collapsed or restructured their organisation, and are still hesitant (or simply unable) to develop new initiatives. Moreover, the concepts and procedures of competitions that have recently applied do not always stimulate or enable architects to participate.

This essay sheds light on recent trends in the management of competitions by clients in the Netherlands, and discusses the implications for architectural firms and the quality of the built environment. It draws on academic and practitioners' literature, reports of Dutch professional institutions, and exemplary cases from interviews with Dutch clients and architects.[1] Trends in Dutch competition concepts, such as more integrated contracts and development competitions, are discussed first. This is followed by trends in the competition procedures, such as the preference for restricted procedures. The essay ends with a discussion of the implications of these trends, and developments in Dutch competition culture.

Trends and developments in Dutch competition concepts

More negotiated procedures and privately contracted jobs

Private clients are generally free to apply the selection procedure that they prefer, but for public clients, this is only allowed in specific situations according to European procurement regulations. These regulations prescribe several procedures that need to be applied when selecting architects. As a result of the implementation of the new Dutch Public Procurement Act in 2012, and slight alterations in the European tendering regulations, negotiated procedures and non-public tenders have become increasingly popular among public clients in the Netherlands.[2] Clients often choose a traditional negotiation procedure with a few potential suppliers in order to limit transaction costs and influence the type of supplier. The trend of fewer publicly announced jobs is demonstrated by a decrease in the number of officially announced tenders over recent years. Privately contracted jobs offer both clients and architects the benefit of a close interaction and specifically chosen discussion items, through which they are better able to secure design quality.

The procedures that can be developed by the client may be as elaborate and time-consuming as the client wishes, but are often quite limited when it comes to facilitating a smooth process. In these situations, the design competition is considered to be too open and elaborate. As a result, we notice that ideas competitions seem to be relatively popular for challenges that have a more open and less urgent character. The concept of the ideas competition offers clients a way of exploring the opportunities of a site without having the obligation to directly sign a contract with the winner. Clients can take along submitted ideas in their development process and organise a European tender at a later stage of the process. In this way, they still utilise the creative potential from the field without real commitments.

Increase in integrated contracts

In the Netherlands, most of the school and cultural facilities are procured in traditional design-bid-build contracts. Sport facilities, infrastructure, housing and urban area developments are generally procured with *integrated* contracts.[3] Over the last two decades, there has been an increase in the number of integrated contracts. Integrated contracts are less complex for clients to handle as there is only a single contracting party. This party takes care of the contracts with all other necessary actors. Popular integrated contracts in the Netherlands are the Design Build (DB) contract and the Design Build Finance Maintain Operate (DBFMO) contract. The first typically selects a contractor, the latter a large consortium of partners that is able to deal with the project's maintenance and/or exploitation for an extensive period of time. DBFMO contracts are mainly applied for large, complex projects, with recent examples, such as the army barracks in Utrecht (Kromhout Kazerne) and the Dutch Supreme Court in The Hague (Hoge Raad der Nederlanden), having contract durations of 25 and 30 years respectively.

The trend towards using more integrated contracts is sometimes seen as a threat to the involvement of an architect and the design quality of the project, as clients look for extensive service delivery rather than architectural value only. Within the consortia that apply for these competitions, the architect usually plays a minor role (for example, producing a preliminary design only), which often results in engineering and construction decisions being made merely on a lowest-price basis. Furthermore, the increase in integrated contracts leads to new parties, such as engineering firms, facility management organisations and specialised contractors, entering the market, which intensifies the competition for architects.[4]

Nevertheless, integrated contracts can also be extremely beneficial for the design quality of the project. Contracting parties, for example, make different decisions regarding the use of materials once they are held responsible for the project's maintenance:

> 'Then you see that you are going to make a different building. Because you are responsible for the window frames the coming 20 years. We apply wooden window frames everywhere, since we don't have to paint them anyway. But now you have to maintain the window frames yourselves. Yes, we then place aluminium, because you don't have to maintain those.'[5]

Some clients explicitly require the inclusion of an architectural firm or party with comparable expertise in the consortium since they aim for unique design quality. For the Dutch Ministry of Finance – one of the first DBFMO projects in the Netherlands – the proposed design was part of the contractual documents to be fulfilled. But also in cases where it is up to the suppliers to compose the consortium, contractors and other firms increasingly invite architects to become a part of their consortium as they notice that the chances of winning increase when an architect is involved. In the exploitation phase of a building, in particular, good design decisions can limit maintenance costs. Sometimes architects even take on a key role in coordinating the quality aspect of the project, as other involved parties don't have the expertise or ambition to oversee the integrative aspects of the construction project

More development competitions

Public clients are increasingly using *development* competitions. By using such competitions, clients mainly target developers or developing contractors to undertake the entire project based on a location that is available.[6] It is yet another practice that outsources the main construction client's responsibilities to private parties and reduces the workforce that is needed within the client organisation. Although the development competition practice may lead to consortia without architectural design firms, contractors and developers increasingly recognise that architects can help them beat the competition by being distinctive.

> *'We won the "Markthal" [a covered marketplace in Rotterdam] in a competition. We also won the "Amsteltoren" [a former office tower in Amsterdam] in a competition. And yes, then you want to be distinctive. So there we had MVRDV and together we brainstorm.'[7]*

Architects also become involved in new roles in relation to these competitions. The preparation of the competition itself, the selection procedure and realisation often require architectural supervision to secure design quality. Clients therefore increasingly hire architects to support them in optimising their plans and assuring design quality. In more complex area developments, clients hire architects to oversee the complete set of multiple parcels, based on different competitions between different sets of consortia. For architects, becoming part of the client organisation is not necessarily a bad thing, since they can strive for design quality themselves. Some architects even try to pursue more of these advisory roles, as they easily lead to additional jobs in the same project, or commissions for other projects.

Trends and developments in Dutch competition procedures

Preference for restricted procedures

Public clients in particular aim to select their architects in a careful manner to ensure the support of their stakeholders and to obey procurement rules. In general, this results in fewer (open) design competitions and more (restricted) tender procedures in the Netherlands. Whether justified or not, clients seem to consider these restricted tender procedures as a means to reduce the risks of budget overruns, planning delays and quality issues – issues which are unfortunately still common in construction projects. Whereas most clients seem to acknowledge that they have a social role in fostering architecture, they also have an increasingly scrutinised public responsibility to create well-functioning and cost-efficient public facilities.[8] Numbers on the website of Architectuur Lokaal,[9] the Dutch support office for design competitions, show that in recent years 90% of all design-related tenders by public clients were EU-restricted tender procedures. Open EU procedures, such as design competitions, represent only 5% of the total of design tenders, of which many are ideas competitions without any follow-up.

Strict procedures

Many public clients are very strict in their interpretation of the EU regulations that apply to architect selections.[10] They often use high, disproportional suitability criteria and time-consuming procedures, which can lead to the exclusion of young architects and small firms from public commissions.[11] The strict procedures and assessment criteria also imply that specific types of assignments, such as schools or healthcare facilities, regularly end up within the same range of firms.

> *'We can never be selected for that because we don't have the right references. We can only participate once the tender specifications are allowing us to submit projects of comparable complexity. But if you are asked to provide five libraries or five city halls ...'[12]*

Clients often include these high selection requirements to avoid potential risks in the development of their projects. The fact that many Dutch clients are merely occasional purchasers, with little experience and knowledge of commissioning architectural services, is possibly one of the underlying reasons for this. Clients don't seem to realise what the impact of their requirements can be for the type of firm that can submit. Depending on the strategies of the architectural firms, this could lead to submissions that can't be executed under the project's conditions, or to firms refusing to participate.[13] Currently, increasing numbers of clients are lowering the financial requirements, or adjusting the conditions for reference projects. This is reinforced by the Dutch Proportionality Guide as part of the current Procurement Act, which provides guidelines for these requirements.

Special criteria for young talent or small firms

To stimulate young talent or small firms, some clients (such as the Dutch Chief Government Architect Office and the municipality of Rotterdam) use selection procedures with limited requirements. They also specifically invite recently established firms to participate in restricted design contests or tenders. Others apply the wildcard method to offer less experienced firms the chance to prove themselves during a competition.

> *'Look, the reason why we were able to win the "Drents Archief" [a Dutch historical museum], for example, is that there was a very active policy of the Central Government [...] that small firms also had to have a chance in European tenders. So the criteria were very basic and on top of that they also divided it into small parcels to reduce the risks.'[14]*

This management practice definitely seems to be paying off in terms of design quality, as the works that are produced by young talent are generally of a very high standard and well received by clients, the general public and the architectural press.[15]

Limited financial compensation

In particular for major public facilities, such as museums and municipal offices, architects are sometimes asked for full design proposals and extensive stakeholder engagements without proper financial compensation.[16] Dutch clients are used to the willingness of architects to participate; even during the global financial crisis architects did not usually complain. Many architectural firms started offering their services below market value, just to get the job and keep their people busy. Firm efforts almost always exceed the compensations that are offered by far:

> *'For example, currently there is a selection for an archival building in Delft – yes it's ridiculous – there you get paid 2,500 euro, VAT included, so that's 1,800 euro; we worked on that for six weeks full time!'[17]*

In the last couple of years, Dutch architects have become more concerned about this issue, and have started protesting against 'cost-draining procedures', either by not participating in competitions[18] or by reaching out to the media.[19] Currently, increasing numbers of public clients are offering financial compensations when firms enter the final round of a competition. Their reimbursements usually don't fully cover the architectural firm's costs, but are enough for firms to be willing to participate. Architects are also increasingly engaging in negotiations with private clients that ask them to participate in an integrated tender or development competition. They make financial arrangements at the start of the tender, such as a fixed compensation, coverage of expenses or a bonus fee once the project is acquired. So far, the limited financial compensations of Dutch clients do not seem to have resulted in reduced design quality. Architects still aim for the highest standard of quality possible, as they don't want to jeopardise their firm's reputation, or their own personal work satisfaction.[20] However, as other countries seem to become increasingly attractive to Dutch architects,[21] limited reimbursements may eventually result in fewer applications from Dutch firms. In such a scenario, the majority of contemporary Dutch architecture may be diffused around the globe, instead of contributing to the identity of Dutch cities.

Conclusion

Trends in the management of Dutch competitions seem to have a strong impact on the potential of architectural firms to participate in competitions or win tenders. Some of the trends facilitate further involvement of the architect; others make things more complicated or create more competition.

The increase in integrated contracts and development competitions in the Netherlands has resulted in a growing number of projects in which architects are commissioned by private firms, such as developing contractors instead of public clients. Although these developments may impact architectural ambitions because of the focus on the overall business case, recent examples also show how architectural value pays off by increasing the chances of winning these types of competitions. At the same time, the total amount of transaction costs increases, because three to five consortia have to submit complete designs for limited financial compensation. The same applies for the restricted tender procedures that are still very popular in the Netherlands.

Architects and construction consortia are increasingly asked to provide crucial parts of their core business – eg their design power – almost for free. This causes friction in the market and could lead to a poorer architecture climate. It could also lead to new opportunities and interesting role changes in traditional supply chains. As a result, a more lucrative competition environment seems indispensable, – in order to ensure high quality designs and a continuation of the Netherlands as breeding ground for Dutch design.

Notes

1 Marina Bos-de Vos, Hans Wamelink and Leentje Volker, 'Trade-Offs in the Value Capture of Architectural Firms: The Significance of Professional Value', in *Construction Management and Economics*, Vol 34, No 1, 2016, 21–34; Marina Bos-de Vos, Leentje Volker and Hans Wamelink, 'Real Estate Development by Architectural Firms: Is the Business Model Future-Proof?', in *Proceedings of the 32nd Annual ARCOM Conference* (Manchester: ARCOM, 2016).

2 *Steunpunt Architectuuropdrachten & Ontwerpwedstrijden, Trends aanbesteden van architectuuropdrachten in Nederland* [Trends in tendering architectural services in the Netherlands] (Amsterdam: Architectuur Lokaal, 2013).

3 *Ibid.*

4 *Ibid.*

5 This quote originates from an interview conducted by one of the authors in January 2015 with a Dutch contractor. The interview is part of the futurA research project on future roles and business models of the architect, see http://www.future-architect.nl.

6 Peter Fisher, Simon Robson and Suzanne Todd, 'The Disposal of Public Sector Sites by "Development Competition"', in *Property Management*, Vol 25, No 4, 2007, 381–99.

7 This quote originates from an interview conducted by one of the authors in January 2015 with a Dutch real estate developer, as part of the futurA project.

8 Leentje Volker and Juriaan van Meel, 'Dutch Design Competitions: Lost in EU Directives? Procurement Issues of Architect Selections in the Netherlands', in *Geographica Helvetica*, No 1, 2011, 24–32.

9 http://www.ontwerpwedstrijden.nl/.

10 Leentje Volker, *Deciding About Design Quality: Value Judgements and Decision Making in the Selection of Architects by Public Clients under European Tendering Regulations* (Leiden: Sidestone Press, 2010).

11 Leentje Volker and Juriaan van Meel, 'Dutch Design Competitions'.

12 This quote originates from an interview conducted by one of the authors in December 2014 with a Dutch architect, as part of the futurA project.

13 Beatrice Manzoni and Leentje Volker, 'Paradoxes and Management Approaches of Competing for Work in Creative Professional Service Firms', in *Scandinavian Journal of Management*, Vol 33, No 1, 2017, 23–35.

14 This quote originates from an interview conducted by one of the authors in January 2014 with an architect-owner of a small Dutch architectural firm, as part of the futurA project.

15 Liesbeth van der Pol et al., *Europa en de architecten – Stand van zaken in de discussie over Europese aanbestedingen van architectendiensten* [Europe and the architects – the state of affairs]. [Den Haag: Ministerie van VROM/Atelier Rijksbouwmeester and Architectuur Lokaal].

16 Leentje Volker and Juriaan van Meel, 'Dutch Design Competitions'.

17 This quote originates from an interview conducted by one the authors in February 2014 with an architect-owner of another small Dutch architectural firm, as part of the futurA project.

18 Piet Vollaard, 2008. Europees Aanbestedingsleed: nu ook met oplossingen [European tendering suffering: now also with solutions] http://www.archined.nl).

19 Atelier Kempe Thill, *Naar een Nieuwe Aanbestedingscultuur – Europees Aanbesteden van Architectendiensten in Nederland* [Towards a new tender culture in the Netherlands], (Rotterdam: Atelier Kempe Thill Architects and Planners, 2008).

20 Marina Bos-de Vos et al., 'Trade-Offs in the Value Capture of Architectural Firms'.

21 Vogels, 'Conjunctuurpeiling BNA, Voorjaar 2015 [Economic Survey BNA, Spring 2015]', BNA (Royal Institute of Dutch Architects), 2015.

CHAPTER 9

PROFESSIONALS WINNING OVER THE COMPETITIONS' SYSTEM

Discussion with Sara Grahn, Stefan Thommen, Angel Borrego Cubero and Cindy Walters

Question (Q): Where does your interest in architectural competitions stem from?

Sara Grahn, White Arkitekter **(SG)**: Even while still at architecture school, I was involved in competitions. The impetus for that still holds true today. With certain competitions, you can apply anonymously, which immediately allows you to be on a level playing field by removing factors that exclude, such as not knowing the client or having the right experience. Competitions can be divided into three categories. The first category, the safe zone, is within the office's field of expertise, where there is a high likelihood of a win. The second category is when we can identify a strategic market and/or client we would like to work with. The first two categories are company initiatives, but the third category is driven by the passion and determination to be awarded a particular 'dream project' through a competition. As an architect, you have to believe that you will be able to give the best answer to the question posted; to have the self-confidence (or even naivety) that you can shape the physical world, creating a better place than it is today.

Stefan Thommen, Annette Gigon / Mike Guyer Architekten **(ST)**: Competitions give us the possibility of exploring a site and making a statement about it; of interpreting it architecturally and 'reflecting' on it. In fact, it was after winning the competition for the Kirchner Museum Davos that we founded our office in 1989, almost 30 years ago. To date, 70–90% of our projects have been the result of competitions we have won. Competitions also give us the opportunity to broaden our field of practice. For example, in 2004 our first office building competition was

Figure 2.10 Prime Tower Office high-rise, Zurich, Switzerland, by Annette Gigon / Mike Guyer Architects, study models

the Prime Tower high-rise in Zurich (see Fig. 2.10), which gave us the chance to work on a larger scale.

Angel Borrego Cubero, OSS Office for Strategic Spaces **(ABC)**: My interest [in architectural competitions] has come in different phases. I had the typical interest [in competitions] as a means of securing work. But the first time I actually looked at them with some intellectual interest was when I was a student. In architectural history classes and books one would learn about some famous competition examples, such as those for the Society of Nations, the Chicago Tribune, etc, revisiting and inadvertently judging again the better known projects. One day, when still a student (in about 1988), *Quaderns* published three losing competition designs by Rem Koolhaas's OMA:

the Très Grande Bibliothèque, the New Town of Mèlun-Sénart and the Zeebrugge Ferry Terminal. It was clear to me, and a lot of my teachers and classmates, that those proposals marked a sea-change in architecture. And these were losing proposals – all three! The same types of historical illustrations that were so didactic with the older competitions suddenly happened in real time. Unexpectedly, a space for thought had been created, not only about architecture design *per se*, but also regarding the social and political tools and technologies that made it possible, one among them being competitions.

A more intense phase of interest began in 2007, when we decided to make a film: a documentary about architectural competitions. At that time I did not have a very deep or precise impression of the field of competitions, but this was changed somewhat through this process.

Cindy Walters, Walters & Cohen **(CW)**: We have always entered competitions as a way of finding work and breaking into new sectors. Our first built project was won through an international design competition, and we have never looked back.

Q: How important have competitions been in your career so far? In how many, and what kinds of, competitions (open/restricted, etc) have you participated to date, and in what capacity? What is the average number of working hours per year that you have invested in competition submissions? How many competition awards have you won to date?

SG: For me, all competitions, but especially those that have successfully led to commissions, have been extremely important for the development of my career and my everyday work. I have participated in a wide variety of competitions: open and invited, national and international, as well as parallel commissions. What probably best characterises the competitions I'm drawn to is a certain complexity, and [that they are] usually within the realm of urban design tasks, public buildings, university buildings and large-scale office buildings. I would estimate that participating in competitions has occupied about a third of my total workload over the years –from being a young architect on the team working full time in the competition project for several weeks to the current situation, where I have the role of project leader and head architect. Nowadays, I work fewer hours on any particular competition; my primary task is more strategic, evaluating the work at critical stages throughout the process. Over the years I have participated in around 25–35 competitions and parallel commissions, and have been awarded about half of them.

ABC: [I have participated] probably in about 50 competitions, the main programmes being housing, cultural, education, office, research and infrastructure. My involvement has varied from that of student collaborator to head architect, with a success rate of a little over 10%. Around 20–25% of office time is spent on competitions.

ST: Since we founded our office in 1989, we have participated in over 200 competitions (invited, restricted and some open competitions) or feasibility studies; 84 of them were awarded, 47 with first prize. The building programmes range from residential buildings, museums, schools and infrastructure-related buildings, as well as offices, to large-scale master plans. Usually, a small team comprising an architect and an intern begins work on a competition project; during the development, the team increases to one or more collaborators, depending on the extent and complexity of the programme.

Per year, we participate in around five competitions, though it can be as many as 12 competitions. Each lasts three to five months, entailing 1,500–3,000 working hours, depending on the procedure.

CW: We enter all types of competitions, from design competitions that require a fully developed design to PQQs and EOIs that require no (or very little) design input. The most common way for us to win new work is through invited, competitive, two-stage competitions where the final selection is made following an interview.

Since 1994, our practice has entered almost 400 open and invited competitions, including contractor, institutional and local authority frameworks, and [we] have won approximately 85 of those. In 2016, the time spent by architects and architectural assistants on competitions was a little more than 2,000 hours; we also have several administrative staff that work on competitions.

Q: What does <u>experimentation</u> mean to you? How do you think the notion of experimentation may be interpreted in architectural terms? Is <u>competition</u> a driving force for experimentation?

CW: One of the specific benefits of competitions is that the process allows one to think and work in ways that are not always possible in everyday practice. We have entered competitions to design building types that we knew nothing about, and the competition process has required us to research and understand the requirements. For example, we were invited to enter a competition to design an office building in the City of London. We were the only practice on a very strong shortlist which had not designed an office building before. We won the competition and

were told afterwards that the client had appreciated our fresh approach.

ABC: Some experimentation happens in competitions. And I think we could do more. But for us, experimentation also happens *outside* competitions. The capacity of a firm to experiment is independent from the format of the commission, and has a lot more to do with the inclination of the firm towards such processes. Competitions can also stifle, or limit, experimentation or innovation, if they are designed that way. Participating architects also often censor themselves in order to produce conventional designs that they feel may be the expected solution for a particular competition. We see a growing danger here. In a way, one of the more pressing and common problems surrounding competitions is the balance between two goods: that of allowing experimentation, and the apparently contrarian one of guiding solutions to accepted good practices, whatever these may be at any given time.

SG: The competition task represents the design process in a very compact and intensive manner. In a very short period of time you have to analyse a brief, formulate goals and strategies, generate ideas and sketches, evaluate them, make decisions, and in the end finalise and represent your idea. The absence of a direct dialogue with the client expedites the process, which means jumping forward to discussing and

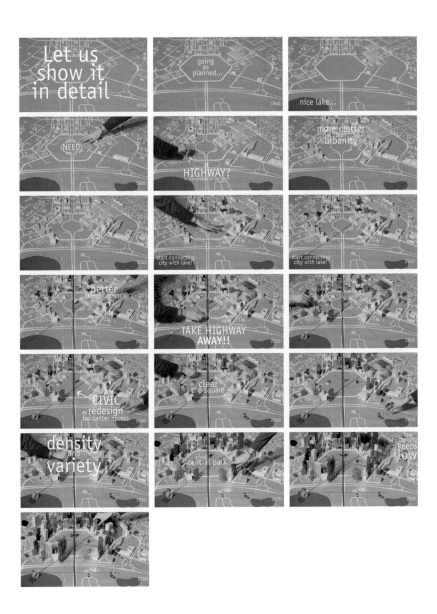

Figures 2.11–2.29 Office for Strategic Spaces
(o-s-s.org) CAPITheticAL competition entry,
Australia, 2012. Stills from video submission.

Figure 2.30 Office for Strategic Spaces (o-s-s.org) CAPITheticAL competition entry, Australia, 2012. Panel 4/4 from printed submission.

testing your ideas on a broader range of professionals within the office at an earlier stage. A vision-based methodology has to be intimately followed by an evidence-based design, where the qualitative aspects of architecture must be quantitatively confirmed from the very early stages of the design. An interdisciplinary methodology – the meeting between disciplines and individuals involved in the competition phase – evokes experimentation. For me, and for White, competitions are used to test and develop our belief in an integrated, sustainable design. All sustainability issues are raised from the start, and clear goals are formulated as a basis for an iterative

design process; architectural ideas are constantly tested in sketches and physical models as well as in simulations and in calculations to improve the design.

ST: A competition is the most important phase of the design process, ie it provides the best opportunity to experiment with different themes – building types as well as materials or construction concepts. That is one of the reasons why we participate in quite a lot of competitions. Certain construction concepts remain on the drawing board over several generations of competitions, and are only put into practice at a later stage, if at all. For example, the subject of 'clothing' buildings with glazed 'curtains' with a wire fabric, used in the Hyatt competition of 1993 (see Fig. 2.31), came to realisation in the Haus Lagerstrasse office building in 2013 (see Fig. 2.32), when a technical solution had been developed.

Q: What is your opinion of competition architecture?

ABC: The field is too large to have just one opinion. If by 'competition architecture' one understands what many critics deride as flashy solutions – usually making no attempt to relate in any way to architectural, social, political or economic context – then it is difficult to be content with the concept. Likewise with experimentation, I believe that this is more the

Figure 2.31
Hotel Park Hyatt, Zurich, Switzerland, by Annette
Gigon / Mike Guyer Architects
Competition model 1993

Figure 2.32
Haus Lagerstrasse office building, Europaallee, Zurich,
Switzerland by Gigon/Guyer Architects. Competition:
2006, second prize, planning/construction: 2007–11

responsibility of the different actors
(promoters, politicians, and of
course the architects themselves)
than it is a result of competition.
Both competitions and direct
commissions have been designed
with such architecture in mind, and
the results are often coherent with
those objectives. If a competition has
not been designed with the idea of
producing a specific kind of flashy,
spectacular object, I have trouble
supposing that an independent panel
of respected professional jurors can
be easily fooled by flashy images and
shapes. This common view seems
to me a little naive, or worse, it shows
too little confidence in the judgment
of peers in a blind process.

ST: Project competitions maintain
a high level of quality. In the best
scenario, a competition is preceded
by discussions, feasibility studies,
etc, establishing parameters within
which participants work. The quality
of competition entries has risen
noticeably in the last 20 years. There
is a tradition of competitions in
Switzerland/Zurich, and the positive

pressure of the competitors – national and international – leads to a high level of good contributions.

What is more, the members of the jury and the client play an important role in this process and the awarded results.

CW: Some of the best buildings in the world have been the result of competitions, but this is more to do with matching good architects with good clients. Competitions can equally well result in bad architecture, where clients or architects (or both) are unclear about the brief, and unrealistic about the limitations of the budget or programme.

SG: I don't know if there is such a thing as 'competition architecture'. In recent years, however, I have noticed a shift of focus onto the *image*, most likely attributed to new ways of communicating architecture through social media. The non-built image is given the same value as the built architectural intervention. A consequence of this contemporary phenomenon might be to move the evaluation of competition entries away from the essence of architecture towards the gesture of architecture. If so, we're facing a common problem in the future of our business.

Q: Is there a competition-generated building that you admire, and that you would like to have designed yourself?

ST: Of course, there are some projects that we would have liked to have realised. But the interesting thing is that some projects give us the opportunity to return to an idea we had been considering in a competition, and develop them further in a next project.

ABC: Quite a lot of them …

CW: I wish we had won the competition for the Tate Modern in London. It is a hugely successful project that has made use of an existing building and given it a new lease of life. It is a London landmark, a cathedral to art, and is visited by millions of people every year.

SG: Without hesitation, my answer is the Library of Alexandria – such a mythological task, beautifully executed by Snøhetta as both a site-specific and symbolic answer to the question posed.

Q: From the competition submissions that you have prepared so far, which is your favourite, and why? Have you built through a competition-generated commission?

ABC: I am fond of quite a lot of them. Not all, but a few. Perhaps with the Civil Registry (Registro Civil) at the Justice Campus of Madrid we were able to change the client's views of what kind of building they needed. It was a surprise result for them as well, and the jury helped them. This was a very innovative administrative

Figures 2.33, 2.34 Office for Strategic Spaces (o-s-s.org) Civil Registry competition. Campus de la Justicia de Madrid, Spain, 2007. Diagrams from second phase and model. Winning entry

Figure 2.35 Oulu housing project. Design: White Arkitekter

and office space project, with a big impact on visitors, which unfortunately got suspended by the recent economic crisis and ensuing political troubles.

SG: I am still very proud of our winning entry for a new housing block at Toppila Shore in Oulu, Finland. For the competition proposal and design of the block, we fully tested and experimented with our sustainable integrated approach, and succeeded. Our ideas and design for a housing block comprising apartments that adapt to the climate throughout the seasons ('Seasons' also became the motto), and responding to the harsh Nordic climate, are still completely valid. Unfortunately, the entry was never built as a result of the global financial crisis in 2008, but the ideas have been developed in other projects, and continue as a red thread in my work and teachings at the School of Architecture in Stockholm.

Figure 2.36 Oulu housing project. 'Seasons' diagram. Design: White Arkitekter

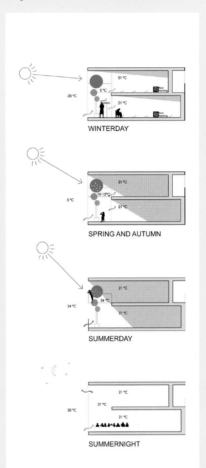

Figure 2.37 Oulu housing project. Wind diagram. Design: White Arkitekter

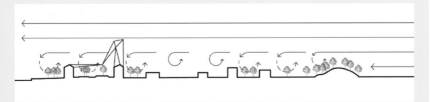

Figures 2.38, 2.39
University building. Design: White Arkitekter

The first project I was part of at White was an open international competition in two stages for a new university south of Stockholm – Södertörn University. We won both competitions, and I continued as a team member for about eight years through implementation. That was a great start to my career, and a good learning experience, going from the initial conceptual ideas at competition phase to seeing the finalised building. A couple of other commissions have gone from competition to realisation, including two finalised master plans. Recently, I have been project-responsible for two newly constructed office buildings north of Stockholm that have their origin in a competition.

CW: My favourite competition win is still our first, which was for a community art gallery in South Africa. The building was delivered on a very small budget, and 20 years on it is still going strong and serving a wide community of emerging young artists. I also loved our submission for the Hepworth Gallery in Wakefield, where we were shortlisted alongside David Chipperfield and Zaha Hadid. I am delighted that David Chipperfield won, and he has designed an extremely good building; but our design made more poetic use of the site.

Figures 2.43, 2.44
Office building. Design: White Arkitekter

Figure 2.40 Walters & Cohen.
The Hepworth Wakefield
competition model

Figure 2.41 Walters & Cohen.
Vajrasana Buddhist Retreat Centre

Figure 2.42 Walters & Cohen.
New Dauntsey House model

Figure 2.45 Extension of Kunstmuseum. Winterthur, Switzerland, by Gigon/Guyer Architects. Competition: 1993, first prize planning/construction: 1994–95

ST: Various projects are interesting and relevant for us in terms of their different aspects; therefore, we have no favourite submission. The museum projects, eg the Kirchner Museum Davos, the extension to the Kunstmuseum Winterthur (see Fig. 2.45), and the Archaeological Museum and Park Kalkriese come to mind (see Fig. 2.46); the Prime Tower in terms of scale; the residential projects in terms of [being] high standard as well as low-cost schemes.

Q: What would your ideal competition brief be, and why?

SG: A well-written brief should include clear hand-in requirements, all available background information and a level of transparency that clearly exposes potential conflicts early on.

ST: A competition brief which allows an architectural contribution, ie an interesting plot and an interesting

Figure 2.46 Archaeological Museum and Park Kalkriese, Osnabrück, Germany. Gigon/ Guyer in collaboration with Zulauf Seippel Schweingruber, Landschaftsarchitekten, Baden. Competition: 1998, first prize planning/construction: 1999–2002

utilisation. A brief which gives us the freedom to experiment, and which is not too restricted with detailed specifications. Moreover, a client who is interested in very good architecture.

ABC: I am more interested in the way competitions are set up, ie what is the organising institution or client, what are their aims, how much thought has gone into [the competition's] preparation, and what is the decision-making process. If

they rate positively on most of these issues, I would usually be happy with the competition.

Something I would like to see much more of in competition briefs is greater freedom for the participants to propose alternatives. Smarter design frameworks and structures would need to be laid out across institutions. For example, it is often the case that too rigid design decisions have been made and approved by democratic bodies before the final design competition, to choose the actual architect in charge before the final proposal is started. Since those initial design decisions have been voted on and passed, it is very difficult to change them, even if this were for the benefit of the city and its inhabitants. It would be advantageous to design these decision processes to be more flexible, while maintaining (and hopefully reinforcing) their political and social legitimacy.

CW: [My ideal competition brief would be] one where we win work in a new sector, meet and get to work with a visionary and ambitious client, and deliver a game-changing building for our client and our practice.

Q: How do you normally find out about new competitions?

ST: Often we are invited to participate in competitions or feasibility studies. Other times, we read about competitions in architectural newsletters and publications, and submit pre-qualification papers. In rare cases, we take part in open competitions.

SG: Through websites or direct invitations.

ABC: Increasingly, we look to institutions with a proven track record of organising good competitions.

CW: Organisers such as RIBA Competitions, Colander and Malcolm Reading Consultants regularly launch suitable competitions, and we are notified via their websites and newsletters. Other opportunities are advertised on institutional, regional, national or continental tender portals, and we receive alerts for these. Finally, and increasingly often, we are invited to participate in competitions run by private clients who have seen or heard about previous projects by Walters & Cohen.

Q: How much have you learned about architectural competitions during your architectural studies?

CW: We participated in a few design competitions as part of our architectural studies but learned nothing about the enormous cost of participating in architectural competitions once in practice.

SG: Ever since I started participating in competitions as a student (and in parallel with my studies), I practised and failed several times, which really became an inclusive part of my education. During internships at some offices here in Stockholm, I was also part of competition processes, gaining yet more professional experience before graduating.

ST: When studying architecture, you are trained to elaborate a convincing architectural idea for a certain plot and a specific task within a few weeks. Competitions are comparable, even though the questions are more precise, and one is already working to an extent in a team with experts.

Q: What advice would you give, with respect to competitions, to someone recently graduated from an architecture school?

ABC: First, to do [competitions] at some other office, for a little while at least. Second, to design for competitions as they would for any other client/commission. Third, to be patient, keep at it, and fight for design competitions to be the standard of public architectural work.

ST: Working on a competition is very important for finding out what really interests an individual in architecture. On the one hand, one can focus on certain aspects, do research on a specific topic, and on the other hand, it offers the possibility to enlarge one's scope. There are so many places and different uses. Therefore, we would definitely advise someone recently graduated to work on competitions.

CW: I would say, they should be selective about the competitions they enter to make sure they have the best chance of winning. See competitions as currency; if they don't win, they still have the opportunity of impressing members of the jury who might remember them next time. They should be prudent about the amount of time and effort they put into competitions, but should do as many as they can afford to do. Be rigorous, ambitious and creative, but remain true to oneself.

SG: Just do it! If they are eager to learn more, and feel in their gut that they just might have the best answer to the posted question, I encourage them to participate in competitions that align with their personal interests and passions, which ultimately becomes translated into positive results!

109

PART

CHAPTER 10

E-PROCUREMENT DELIVERING BETTER DESIGN COMPETITIONS

Walter Menteth

Introduction

A key question in the built environment is how society acquires best architectural quality appropriately, and at good value, and how architects best serve and engage these needs sustainably. In public architectural competitions, the successful relationship between delivery and end product, and the alignment of processes, briefs and parties are recognised to be significant factors in unlocking better value and opportunities. For all design professionals as practical stakeholders, it's equally important when competing to win work that they consider that it is won fairly, on design merit, is well briefed and is capable of delivering our culture, clients and industry the best value sustainable architecture.

This architectural culture is profoundly determined by the strategic policy and regulatory framework of public competitions, which practising architects have generally failed to fully engage. In these, a lack of clarity and transparency, along with excessive time, cost and complexity, have contributed to disenfranchisement and disillusionment, and to the alienation from the processes of so many among society, clients and industry. If progress is to be delivered, and better environmental outcomes achieved from public architectural competitions, then fuller and more proactive engagement is required, with better facilitation of the means to achieve this.

Context

As they have wide scope covering works, supplies and services, are applied across different jurisdictions, sectors and values, and relate to other international and national commercial competitions policy, the public competitions directives and national regulations are inevitably complex. And understanding competition regulations, procedures and requirements has been identified as a significant problem. The frequently needless over-application of requirements (leading to unnecessary information requests, unduly onerous conditions and bad practices) that increases inefficiencies and pointlessly excludes competitors – known as 'gold-plating' – has also been heavily criticised. Evidently, this ailment is particularly acute in the UK.[1]

Research had also revealed other damaging impacts from legislation on competition policy. It had been found that in many cases the proscriptive detail has resulted in impacts quite the opposite to the core principles of the EU treaties. In competitive procedures, for example, it was shown that small and medium-sized enterprises (SMEs) were being discriminated against in access to competitions; costs were being wasted; competition was being adversely reduced; growth was being restrained (which was reducing EU construction capacity), so that best value wasn't being achieved.

In response to these considerations a number of significant reforms were called for, and introduced (Directive 2014/24/EU[2] and PCR 2015 [3]),but despite these, a 'one size fits all' approach still dominates, and the reforms introduced were insufficient, particularly for achieving the principle of proportionality specified within the EU treaties. This strategic imperative had been sought by UK architects,[4] while the Netherlands also developed responses in its revised national guidance[5]; but this was not sufficiently embraced by the national governments at EU level. Of equal importance, the need to fundamentally address the values at which the WTO thresholds are set – with more consideration given to further reforming structures, the scope of regulations and their proscriptions – was identified, to achieve better balance between competing interests, sectors, scales and types of delivery.

Nevertheless, the EU competition reforms of 2014 provided certain welcome changes, delivering some potential innovations that may contribute to improving architectural culture. The ongoing challenges have therefore shifted towards embedding the available opportunities, and doing so facilitated by new digital technology.

BIM (Building Information Modelling), e-invoicing and the protocols necessary to establish open cross-platform interoperability have so far been the main emphasis in emerging digital opportunities in architecture, much of which is concentrated on post-competition outputs relating to production, project programmes, financial management and coordination. By comparison, there has been little attention paid to early stage pre-competition and tendering process activity, and consultants' appointments, which might contribute to better resolving reported problems in the preparation of a client's brief, access to competitions, procedural costs, selections, complexity, efficiency, effectiveness, and professionalising and improving knowledge and guidance. It is notable that even less has been done in this field by those having any professional architectural design experience, who might contribute valuable insights.

E-procurement, however, sustained by many new provisions within the EU public contract directives, now offers exciting possibilities for improving architectural competition practice. E-procurement can be used innovatively for improving delivery of social and economic betterment; for effectiveness and efficiency; for the dissemination of knowledge, raising skills and improving practices; and for increasing participation, engagement and discourse while gathering further research evidence for appraising impacts that allows for further policy reform in future.

Project Compass CIC

Some of this emerging potential is explored in the architectural sector through an extensive range of digital competition support and intelligence services now being provided by Project Compass CIC, which is a voluntary sector-specific non-profit organisation, established in 2013 by four UK architects. It provides a range of functions largely delivered through its free-to-use website.[6] Its objectives are to make competitions more transparent, accessible, effective and efficient, of higher quality, better value and more professional. Its aim is 'Better Procurement: Better Design'!

Following on from their preceding research, the Project Compass directors formed an early European collaboration with Architectuur Lokaal in the Netherlands, whose Steunpunt digital helpdesk had impressed with its ability to address pragmatically many identified UK issues. This collaboration enabled a degree of forward systems integration, comparative data analysis and mutual support, and opened up further cross-border opportunities. The Project Compass interface and tab headings partially mimicked the established Steunpunt to provide a degree of standardisation, delivering user familiarity internationally.

Fulcrum

For public UK architectural competitions, the Project Compass portal homepage, called Fulcrum, now supplies the first free Official Journal of the European Union (OJEU) notice service that delivers mobile and desktop competition notifications, with RSS, Twitter and calendar feeds also available. The Fulcrum page (see Fig. 3.1) presents a Rolodex-style display which is coloured and ordered according to the time remaining that is available for bidders to compete, from green through to red. The page is interactive, and can be scrolled through to readily reveal other notices; filtering can be set easily, and the time to make a bid submission is clear.

This UK service digitally captures and filters OJEU notices, which are further refined by scripts that audit the data and text, and capture outliers. The European Commission retains public access to notices dating back five years, so this has also been acquired, allowing the platform to mine all the data provided from these competition notices, and permitting further data extrapolations to be automatically captured, ordered and digitally stored. Some of this data is then selected and publicly presented on the portal's Sesame webpage.

Figure 3.1 Fulcrum front page of the Project Compass portal

Sesame

The information in Sesame covers notices and awards, clients, competitors and tenders by type of procedure, building type, region, award criteria, values, numbers of bids, bid stages, etc, and is displayed in tabulated and graphic visualisations, in real time. Although typically only five years' worth are publicly displayed, the Sesame database contains records of more than 15,404 OJEU notices as well as 40,752 individual awards published since 24 October 2008.

Research had found a number of issues with access to UK competitions,[7] with similar accessibility issues found at EU level[8]; it also found that a large number of professionals remained completely unaware that information on public competitions was even freely available. Within the UK, companies instead offer extraction, and search and filtering facilities, delivering summary competition recommendations to likely bidders for a cost which can start at £750 a year. To access competition notices establishes a paywall.

Wherever there are paywalls restraining bidders from being able to access and evaluate a competition, or make a submission, then evidentially engagement by small businesses in competitive procedures falls.[9] The issue of public access paywalls was addressed by specifying that commissioners make all documents and participation free (Directive 2014/24/EU), but competitions' bidders still needed access to fully appraise competition notices, the relevant briefs and all associated documentation to determine their potential, the conditions and their own suitability to participate. The Fulcrum service now provides open access to these opportunities, which contributes significantly to addressing these well-documented issues.

Compass

The Project Compass service also contains a range of resources under its Compass tab which covers its digital guidance. This includes information about directives, the national public contract regulations, government guidance, and guidance on the application, as well as sources of other information and international competition portals.

Publications

Under the Publications tab on the Project Compass portal, a range of procurement-related publications are disseminated. The Publications portal has been used to report on both general and specific issues, and provide guidance on competition and practice, as well as the salient challenges of poor procurement practices. Some have been issued to highlight significant competition irregularities where avowed policy or regulations have not been complied with, for example (see Fig. 3.2) in the awarding of contracts under the Education Funding Agency national frameworks,[10] while others such as the Project Compass *Design Contest Guidance*[11] have addressed specific procurement procedures for architectural services, with best practice recommendations, guidance and innovations.

As it has been possible for Project Compass to research UK public architectural competitions on OJEU in sufficient detail from the extensive data now being captured for the first time, these findings have also been published. This provides new insights into UK procurement practices, their processes, distribution, typologies, the appointments made, trends and forecasts, the market spreads, efficiencies and effectiveness. A comprehensive analysis of these issues and their trends has been released, in the first of an anticipated series of publications, which will allow the impacts of reforms to date to be monitored and reported upon over time.[12] This significantly improves transparency and knowledge.

Interventions

In specific architectural procurements, Project Compass CIC has intervened to seek amendments in support of practical improvements, and has now been engaged in representing the profession and industry in over 25 such cases across the UK and Ireland. Project Compass's pivotal analysis and reporting on the subject of the flawed procurements for London's notorious Thames Garden Bridge has also significantly contributed to raising knowledge about competitive procedures more widely among the UK public.[13]

International collaboration

TheFulcrum.eu portal

The Project Compass Fulcrum and Sesame services, however, are only part of the fully integrated independent TheFulcrum.eu portal,[14] also accessible through links on both the Project Compass and Steunpunt websites. TheFulcrum.eu portal is a unique digital international architectural competitions facility, developed in collaboration between Project Compass in the UK and Architectuur Lokaal in the Netherlands.

Put simply, the portal gathers the notices from the two countries into one location, on a single portal. This merging of data onto the portal is done automatically using agreed protocols. The UK and Dutch back-office programming and structures are, however, different. While the digitally automated programming of Project Compass's Fulcrum service avoids most of the manual curation required by Steunpunt (because it is curated before uploading), Steunpunt can more readily also capture works below EU threshold values. TheFulcrum.eu service provides a separate open access portal delivering public competition notices from both countries, offering further tools and analytical data, contributing to increasing transparency and efficiencies, and stimulating cross-border trade, while also providing a platform offering the potential for many future collaborative opportunities, and a forum for promulgating best practices internationally.

TheFulcrum.eu network partners also have a data-sharing agreement allowing them access to comparative cross-border competitions research, backed by fine-grained data; it enables those – be they clients, or architects in either (or any) country – to research and interrogate notices directly through the interface.

TheFulcrum.eu network is a unique cross-border collaboration, cooperation, integration and innovation by independent non-profit organisations. The structure of this federated network allows these organisations the opportunity to pursue and develop their own initiatives, approaches and outputs in response to their own national contexts, while sharing salient components of their functionality and data. TheFulcrum.eu strategy has been structured specifically as an open, collegiate and scalable network offering an international digital platform. Other countries are now being welcomed and invited to join if represented by an independent, non-commercial legal entity.

Competitions

The facilities of the Project Compass platform have also now been used for pre-procurement activities and competition procedures having more direct practical applications. The Portsmouth Elephant Cage contest, undertaken in collaboration with Architectuur Lokaal through TheFulcrum.eu network, is an example.[15] This innovative open design contest competitive call was for 18 UK and Dutch architects, landscape architects and engineers. Selection into collaborative professionally integrated teams was then made for the purpose of exploring issues relating to climate change resilience and sea defence strategies along 6km of the exposed Portsmouth–Southsea coastal frontage, and successfully informing forward integrated design strategies for the £65m coastal defence works being proposed there. This work drew on the partners' collaboration and experiences of innovative competitive practices, and was organised and facilitated through their digital services.

Reach

Between the digital launch of Project Compass in April 2015 and December 2016, the website attracted over 89,902 page views, 31,509 site visits and 23,019 visitors, with over 1,324 unique views of two popular publications, *Design Contest Guidance* and *Thames Garden Bridge*[16] (both also disseminated through other means). In addition, 3,422 tweets have disseminated competition notices and information. The service's value is being increasingly recognised, with usage and return visitors steadily rising. Project Compass outputs have now also been extensively cited in the professional press, the national press, the Greater London Assembly, Houses of Parliament and elsewhere. TheFulcrum. eu website has attracted over 39,000 visitors, who visited the site over 90,000 times in its first 18 months.

Figure 3.2 The digital platforms have hosted various additional productions

New departures

Project Compass has been developing a unique digital tool, delivering an ambitious new bespoke UK e-procurement service which will provide, from inception to completion, an online interactive competition service for architectural procedures. This will be located on its portal on the Compass tab and provide a Work Implementation Platform (WIP).

In the first phase, a free digital service for design contest competitive procedures is projected, which is perceived to be of equal value to both private and public clients. The aim is to transform this procurement route, take the opportunity to expand an identifiable gap in the market, advance design quality competitive selection, and better align UK procedures with a large number of reported recommendations.[17] In this online competition service the logical structures and processes of the public directives and regulations have been mapped and digitalised.

A staged digital methodology is provided to prepare, write, publish and issue an architectural competition procedure along with all requisite notices and the management and running of the process. This WIP is structured around a simple sequence of interrogative questions and assessment methodologies, which clients are asked to consider and respond to, with online guidance and recommendations to support their appraisals. Language and operations are kept simple – in plain English, and as straightforward as possible.

A kernel forming part of the supporting guidance has already been largely issued as a separate and standalone publication (see Fig. 3.2).[18] This guidance may also be used simply to provide prior insight for clients, providing valuable transparency and allowing them to more fully appraise the suitability of a procedure and recommended practices.

Following initial set-up, registration and some interrogative stages, a digital repository is provided to clients for gathering together relevant competition documentation in a secure cloud service. For defining project-specific requirements, online guidance and advice is made available, including how and when it is appropriate to appoint competition programmers, a contest secretary, the jury assessors, etc.

The process can only be certified as complete and compliant upon adherence to the recommended requirements. On completion of the pre-competition stage, a contest notice is automatically filled in, registered and lodged on OJEU for issue, along with an automatically generated website to contain data from the preceding completed stages and the repositories, along with any other required documentation. The appearance of this secure site can be customised for the project by the client or user.

The client's/user's individual site will then deliver functionality over the duration of all competition stages, for live transactions, and the issue of pre-collated briefs, terms, conditions, programmes, registration and submission, with managerial templates, etc, providing a virtual forum in which the competition may be held. This facility is constructed to be extendable and scalable. New kernels can be embodied which will enable feedback, archiving and analysis of exemplars, which can inform new and better practice, as stakeholders will be requested to make selected information publicly available.

Typically, to organise a very minor UK design contest currently costs clients upwards of £40,000 from existing providers, while costs for recent international competitions have been over £1m.[19] This WIP removes many barriers to expanding the market for use of design contests in both the private and public sectors, with 75% cost efficiencies projected.

Along with opening up opportunities for design contests, this contributes to greater transparency, effectiveness and efficiency through digital standardisation. The aim is also to deliver more professional and intelligent procurement practices by allowing competition programmers the opportunity to better address qualitative, contextual and project-specific briefing, unencumbered; shifting emphasis from procedures to the vision and ambitions upon which the commission should be based, without recourse to early specialist advice or external consultancy. This service will contribute to returning decisions on many competition questions closer to stakeholders, the public and end users, by putting greater control of the competition process in their hands.

Conclusion

The Project Compass services now supply public clients, industry and architects with a range of valued innovations and facilities. In the long term, however, the real benefit of this systemic approach lies in the data which permits clear comparative trends and progressions to be evidenced and reported, and the progress of reform to be evaluated. This provides invaluable feedback and intelligence to further inform future policy and practice.

Notes

1 Prepared for the European Commission by PWC, London Economics, and Ecorys Research and Consulting, 'Public Procurement in Europe: Cost and Effectiveness', March 2011 (Fig. 1.23; Fig. 2.12; Fig. 2.46).

2 Directive 2014/24/EU of the European Parliament and of the European Council on Public Procurement, and repealing Directive 2004/18/EC. European Parliament, Council of the European Union, in Official Journal of the European Union, February 2014.

3 The Public Contract Regulations 2015 (England, Wales and Northern Ireland) enacted 26 February 2015. Available at: http://www.legislation.gov.uk/uksi/2015/contents/made.

4 *Building Ladders of Opportunity: How Reforming Construction Procurement can Drive Growth in the UK Economy* (London: RIBA, 2012), 34.

5 *Schrijfgroep Gids Proportionaliteit Piano 1e herziening*, April 2016. http://www.pianoo.nl/regelgeving/gewijzigde-aanbestedingswet-2012/herziene-gids-proportionaliteit.

6 Project Compass website 2016. http://www. projectcompass.co.uk/index.php.

7 *Building Ladders of Opportunity*.

8 Paulo Boffo, Walter Menteth et al., *European Competition Programmer Handbook: GreenArch Project Results with Summary Recommendations*, The GreenArch EU Project, 2015. 41. DOI: 10.13140/RG.2.1.3544.0722.

9 Walter Menteth, EU green paper on the modernisation of EU public procurement policy: towards a more efficient European procurement market: response paper. Walter Menteth Architects, on behalf of RIBA Small Practices Group, March 2011, 17–19. RIBA Procurement Case Studies (London: RIBA, 2012) (appendix 13.10 and 13.12 p.26) (http://www.architecture.com/files/ribaholdings/policyandinternationalrelations/policy/publicaffairs/2012/procurementcasestudies.pdf).

10 Walter Menteth, Roger Newman and Paul Bogle, *Education Funding Agency Procurement Issues* (London: Project Compass CIC, 2015). National Federation of Builders, DeNové and Project Compass CIC, March 2015. DOI: 10.13140/RG.2.2.35648.33284.

11 Walter Menteth et al., *Design Contest Guidance: For Selecting Architects and Design Teams* (London: Project Compass CIC, 2015).

12 Walter Menteth et al., *Public Construction Procurement Trends 2009–2014* (London: Project Compass CIC, 2014).

13 Walter Menteth. *Thames Garden Bridge: Procurement Issues* (London: Project Compass CIC, 2016). DOI: 10.13140/RG.2.1.3955.6883.

14 Project Compass CIC, Architectuur Lokaal. TheFulcrum.eu. http://www.thefulcrum.eu.

15 The Portsmouth Elephant Cage. http://www. elephantcage.projectcompass.co.uk/. Ibid, 13.

16 Ibid.

17 ACE (Architects' Council of Europe). *European Public Procurement Legislation and Architects' Services: Recommendations and Guidelines for Transposition into National Law*. Adopted by the ACE General Assembly on 24 April 2014; 4, 5, 8, 14, 15. http://www.ace-cae.eu/77/. Menteth et al., *Public Construction Procurement Trends 2009–2014*, 24–27. *Building Ladders of Opportunity*, 21, 22. Rec.1.4.3).

18 Walter Menteth et al., *Design Contest Guidance*.

19 For confidentiality – sources undisclosed.

CHAPTER 11

BIM: A DISCUSSION IN NORWEGIAN COMPETITIONS

Birgitte Sauge

Digitisation and technological advances in building design and industry have enabled new possibilities for the architectural design process, the administration of the building process, building maintenance and the globalised building industry. Furthermore, some architects have engaged proactively in the creation and use of digital tools to achieve results that would not otherwise be possible to attain.[1] The efficiency of computer-aided design (CAD) software and the high level of digital skills of today's young generation of architects means that an increasing part of the design process is executed in digital 3D models.[2] As part of this recent trend, Building Information Modelling (BIM) has been introduced. In everyday language, BIM can be defined as a geometric model connected to a database, containing information about (and relations between) the objects that constitute the represented building. The main purpose of BIM is to share information in order to facilitate efficient cooperation between different skills engaged in the planning and building process, and afterwards, during the maintenance of the building.[3] BIM comes in different formats, but the most used standardised open file format is Industry Foundation Classes (IFC).[4]

In Norway, BIM was introduced in 2005, and since 2011 has been mandatory for all building projects commissioned by the Directorate of Public Construction and Property (Statsbygg), the largest public client in Norway.[5] To Statsbygg, BIM is an efficient tool that helps make planning and construction processes efficient, thus reducing costs. According to Statsbygg, BIM helps to ensure that a building is 'buildable'.[6]

This essay concentrates on one particular aspect of the digitisation of architectural practice – the use and value of BIM in open architectural competitions. Central to this are investigations around how BIM is bound up in processes within the competition institution, thereby reconfiguring these practices, as exemplified by the recent open planning and design competition for the new Viking Age Museum in Oslo. The focus is on how BIM is understood, interpreted and negotiated in design-evaluation processes, in relation to the material submitted by the architects.[7]

BIM in competitions

Since 2009, BIM has been a requirement in open planning and design competitions directed by Statsbygg. Since then, BIM has been required in less than a handful of open competitions, but in many limited competitions. This distinction has arisen partly because open planning and design competitions are no longer much used as a procurement process, and partly because of the general workload caused by open competitions, and the workload connected to BIM in particular.[8] As part of the submitted entries in each competition, architects must provide a BIM worked out by a suitable object-based BIM/CAD program in IFC format, according to a list of specifications in the brief. Statsbygg's reasons for including BIM in programmes for open competitions are manifold. The main strategy is to identify architects with competence in digital modelling. BIM allows the competition support and the staff of Statsbygg to study the visualisations of the location of the project on the site, as well as specific characteristics and sightlines, geometric forms and volumes, and functionality. It also enables visualisation of the main materials, and the construction and climate solutions. BIM also permits 4D progress control tables, information generated from quantities lists and thereby analyses of the economics of the submission. According to Statsbygg, other advantages with BIM in the competition context include the possibility to control that requirements set in the brief and the submitted entry match, and to print models. Representatives from Statsbygg stress that BIM is not meant for expressing (and thereby evaluating) architectural features such as facades, materiality, colour and light. These features are supposed to be expressed by the illustrations and the text on the panels.[9]

Open planning and design competition for architects and landscape architects: Viking Age Museum, University of Oslo, Oslo, Norway

In addition to the uniqueness of the task and the interest of the winning entries, the digital aspects and the debate about BIM raised among Norwegian architects make the Viking Age Museum competition worth studying. The competition was announced on 4 September 2015, with a submission deadline of 2 December 2015. Statsbygg was in charge of both the preparation and implementation of the competition process. The competition followed the current practice according to agreements with the National Association of Norwegian Architects (NAL), Norwegian legislation and European standards.[10]

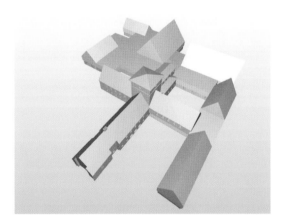

Figure 3.3 Atelier Oslo A/S, motto 'Slektskap'. Image from BIM model, the Viking Age Museum, Oslo, Norway, 2016 (image from Solibri Model Viewer)

The brief asked for design proposals for a new addition (9,300m²) to the existing Viking museum, and the programme included spaces for exhibitions as well as educational and engaging activities for a large number of visitors (minimum 500,000 a year), offices and workshops, and public areas. The brief also asked for proposals for four types of exhibition displays (an icon trail, an in-depth show, activity zones and special exhibits).

The jury of the Viking Age Museum competition included nine members. The client, Statsbygg, was represented by the director of the Department of Strategies and Development, cand.oecon[11] by education, an architect and an engineer from the staff. The user, the University of Oslo/Museum of Cultural History, was represented by an architect and the director of the Museum of Cultural History (an archaeologist). The architects were represented by an architect and a landscape architect, appointed by their associations. An architect appointed by the Swedish architects' association, and a curator and scholar on the Viking Age from the British Museum, represented the international community of peers.

In addition to the originality of the design concept and architectural quality, the criteria for the evaluation of the submitted entries were (in non-priority order) as follows: feasibility, cultural heritage considerations, exhibition concept and environmental solutions. The final winning entry was to be announced after a negotiation procedure among the three winning teams, according to public procurement regulations.

It is worth noting that the communication between Statsbygg and the competitors was nearly 100% digital (except for one information meeting) – from the invitation published on Statsbygg's website (which contained, among other things, digital maps, BIM requirements and 3D models) through to the submission of the architects' entries (six panels in PDF format and a BIM) via a webhost, and finally to the digital exhibition and presentation of the winning entries on Statsbygg's website.

Contestants were required to submit a landscape plan (1:500), floor plans with the sections marked, and associated information about the proposed exhibitions and the links between them and the outdoor area (1:200) and sections (1:200), as well as a minimum of three perspectives from three given standpoints. Contestants were also required to submit a short text about the project, an overview of the total area and volume, and a BIM.

One hundred and nineteen participants of various nationalities registered and gained access to Statsbygg's database: 71 Norwegians, three Swedes, 15 Danes and 30 non-Scandinavians, among them five from the UK. One hundred and sixteen entries were submitted. Five entries were rejected; four of them for not submitting appropriate BIMs.[12] That meant that 111 firms succeeded in submitting BIMs. The total number of entries may have seemed low to some, with comparisons being made in discussion to the international competition for the National Opera and Ballet in Oslo in 2000, which attracted 242 entries, and the National Museum in Oslo in 2009, which attracted 237 entries. In the competition for Guggenheim Helsinki in 2014 a total of 1,715 entries were submitted.[13] The president of NAL, Alexandria Algard, attributed the relatively low number of entries to the requirement of a BIM as part of the entry.[14] A debate among architects followed in the newspapers and in NAL's internal newsletter and Facebook page. The actual need for a BIM, and the level of detail represented in a BIM in the early phases of the design process, and in a planning and design competition in particular, was the main topic. Other reflections dealt with architects' IT skills in general, and the amount of non-compensated time and resources invested by a large group of competing architects. Interestingly, the rest of the competition's digital aspects raised no debate.

Hypothesis, main research questions, analytical perspectives and some findings

One hypothesis derived from the debate was the fear among architects that BIM contributes to a recent trend, which reduces the importance of the architect's role and competence as expert members of the jury in open planning and design competitions. Hence, the focus of this analysis is on understanding what BIM represents in the competition context (as opposed to the traditionally required submission material) on one hand, and whether there is a connection between the inclusion of BIM as a submission requirement and the evaluation of the entries on the other. To be specific, the analysis focuses on whether BIM represents a movement towards rewarding criteria such as functionality and feasibility, rather than the overall design concept given in the proposed building, ie whether digitisation (and BIM in particular) reflects a break with the more or less homogenous 150-year-old tradition of graphic representations and evaluation in architecture competitions.[15]

Interviews with a small selection of the 111 competing architect teams reflected a dual situation regarding how digital media and BIM were incorporated into the design process and the final entries.[16] For example, one office made all the illustrations for their competition entry in the CAD program used for all their projects, in combination with free-hand drawings of particular details. When the design process was finished, a young freelance architect transferred the project to the BIM/IFC format.[17] One office commissioned two of the main perspectives from a professional rendering firm.[18] The majority of the offices made the required BIM in-house, as part of the design process. As a result, IT competence in general (and BIM competence in particular) is high, but differentiated among the contestants.

What about the competence, skills and literacy of the members of the jury? Interviews revealed different types of knowledge and experience with architecture and architectural competitions within the jury.

Five of the nine members of the jury were architects, with knowledge about BIM through their practice. Whether all of them had practical experience with BIM is questionable. The rest of the members had probably very little (if any) experience with BIM. Nonetheless, the representative of the Museum of Cultural History – who had no former experience with architectural competitions – claimed that his personal competence and professional background made it relatively easy for him to participate in the jury: 'As an archaeologist, I am used to working in plans and sections, and we experiment with digital media in our research and exhibitions.' The use of digital media was not a barrier. This individual was also positive about the distribution of the panels in a digital format by memory stick to all jury members. However, the files did not work on his laptop: 'The size of the files was too large for the capacity of the hardware. And the dynamic interface of the 3D model was not working properly.'[19] Besides, the graphical capacity of the laptop was insufficient. As a result, in order to understand the projects, this individual worked with A3 prints, downsized files and on servers.

We can conclude that the general competence of the jury was fairly high on architectural competitions, as was their IT competence, and that the architects represented some expert knowledge on BIM, as opposed to the lay members in the jury.

Figure 3.4 From the jury room. Two of the four large screens surrounding the jury's meeting table.

The digital media and requirements also influenced the jury meetings, and the way the evaluation was conducted. The meetings took place in a room with four large screens. That made it possible to view, for example, four panels at the same time, or to view BIM next to three panels. It also allowed the jury to compare different projects and to have presentations by external experts. A dedicated group of staff (the competition secretariat/support, among them IT specialists) manoeuvred the jury through a specially tailored BIM viewer.

The interviewees in the study gave the impression that this use of BIM functioned very well. According to one of the lay members of in the jury, BIM functioned best as a basis for discussion concerning the most interesting projects: to illustrate how the proposed buildings were situated, and how the layout of the interiors functioned, for example. 'Using BIM on my own was not that rewarding', he added.[20] Conversely, one of the representatives of the architects stated that BIM was not important for the evaluation in a planning and design competition: 'The architect's understanding of the assignment in the sense of both culture and technology is expressed in the visualisations, and hence represents the project's standards.'[21] These statements clearly express the difference between the expert and the lay members, but also reveal the crucial importance of the mediating role of the competition support, a role that has not been that clear in former analyses of competition practice.

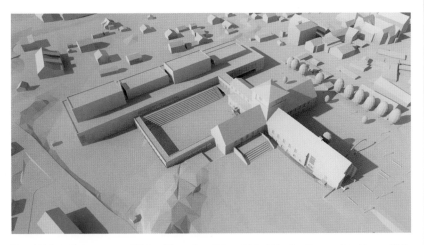

Figure 3.5 div.A arkitekter as, motto "På slaget", image from BIM model, the Viking Age Museum, Oslo, Norway, 2016

What about the submitted competition panels; how do they reflect the digitisation of the design process and the intentions of the architects? What do they represent (as opposed to the BIMs) with regard to the evaluation of the entries?

In the submitted entries, the architects made use of all available techniques: basic 2D digital images, drawings by hand that have been digitally manipulated, digital perspectives and axonometric sketches – some of them included detailed hand-drawn additions illustrating both how things should be built and what they should look like, as well as stills of 3D models. Written texts and various tables of areas were included in the panels. Together, visual images, texts and overall composition through the panels and BIM constituted a narrative of the proposed building. It is worth noting that facades do not appear as a request in the brief, and hence are not in the panels. Yet one of the participating architects stated that the general layout of the various panels had not changed at all since the introduction of digital media: the format was the same (A1) and the type and scale of drawings the same.[22]

In literature, it is argued that the architect's intention with orthographic projections is to create an image which is objective and true as a realistic representation of the building, as opposed to intentionally subjective and persuasive perspective images, as a kind of favourable representation.[23] It is argued that 'objective' and 'subjective' are not qualities inherent in the actual representation of the proposed building; rather they are linked to the viewer's perception and interpretation of the representation as 'true' or 'persuasive'.[24]

This study examines whether digital modelling has changed the understanding of architectural representations. From daily life we get the impression that lay people tend to interpret digital renderings as persuasive, as a kind of unreal vision. What about BIM? Is BIM considered an objective or persuasive type of representation? Interestingly, it seems like the majority of the jury members, across their competence, interpret BIM as a neutral representation of a proposed building. It may be argued that, as well as the traditional orthographic representations, BIM is open to different types of interpretations according to the actual reader and the context. The study so far indicates that the IT competence of the jury members, together with the competence and role of the competition support and external experts, make strong prerequisites concerning the perception of BIM and its role in the evaluation process. In this sense, the study sheds light on the discourse, and on the tensions and negotiations concerning the interpretation of BIM. Whether BIM was used mainly for controlling the proposed areas and costs as described in Statsbygg's strategy, or also for evaluation of the main architectural features of the building's concept, remains moot. Both uses relate to the overall evaluation criteria – originality and architectural quality of the design concept, feasibility, cultural heritage considerations, exhibition concept and environmental solutions – but the understanding and weighting of the criteria may differ, and thus lead to different conclusions.

Notes

1 Mirko Zardini, 'Archaeologists of the Digital – Some Field Notes', in *Archaeology of the Digital – Field Notes – Projects Files: Peter Eisenman, Frank Gehry, Chuck Hoberman, Shoei Yoh*, ed. Lynn Grey (Montreal: Canadian Centre for Architecture, Sternberg Press, 2013), 6.

2 *The Digital Turn in Architecture 1992–2012* gives a good introduction to the development. *The Digital Turn in Architecture 1992–2012*, AD Reader, ed. Mario Carpo (London: John Wiley & Sons Ltd, 2013).

3 Richard Garber, 'Optimisation Stories: The Impact of Building Information Modelling on Contemporary Design Practice', in *The Digital Turn in Architecture 1992–2012*, 226–239.

4 http://www.en.wikipedia.org/wiki/Building_information_modeling.

5 I have not made a survey of the prevalence of BIM, but today's architects in the United States, United Kingdom, the Netherlands, Norway and Finland are familiar with the use of BIM in large commissions.

6 http://www.statsbygg.no/Oppgaver/Bygging/BIM/.

7 This study is a work in progress, bound up in my ongoing research project entitled 'Architecture Museums and Digital Design Media'. The project is part of 'MEDIASCAPES – Cultural Heritage Mediascapes: Innovation in Knowledge and Mediation Practices', running from 2015–19, financed by the Norwegian Research Council.

8 The first open competition with BIM requirement was the National Museum of Art, Architecture and Design. Representatives from Statsbygg and the architects' associations are currently evaluating the inclusion of BIM in competitions.

9 Competition support, presentation dated 25 October 2016.

10 Competition programme, version 1.2, 23 September 2016. http://www.statsbygg.no/Prosjekter-og-eiendommer/Byggeprosjekter/Vikingtidsmuseet/Konkurransen/.

11 cand.oecon is an academic degree in economics, equivalent to a Master of Economics.

12 The rejected contestants (of both Norwegian and foreign origin) had submitted a digital model with only spatial objects. Statsbygg staff email, 9 August 2016.

13 Mikael Godø, 'Holmgang om BIM' in *Arkitektnytt 2016*, No 2, 16.

14 *Aftenposten*, 5 December 2015.

15 In the open architecture competition as an institutionalised practice the focus has been on the main idea and concept (situation on the site, volumes and organisation of rooms) of the proposals, represented through orthographic drawings such as situation plans, floor plans, sections, facades and perspectives. Additional texts explained the proposed materials, construction and estimated costs. Birgitte Sauge, 'Arkitekturtegning og kontekst. Arkitektkonkurransen om Norges Rederforbunds bygning, 1930', thesis, University of Bergen, 2003.

16 The interviewees included some of the awarded firms and the two firms that are partners in the Mediascapes research project.

17 Interview by the author, 30 June 2016.

18 Interview by the author, 10 August 2016.

19 Email, 8 August 2016.

20 Interview by the author, 8 August 2016.

21 Interview by the author, 3 August 2016.

22 Interview by the author, 30 June 2016.

23 These concepts relate to the modus concept borrowed from rhetoric.

24 Birgitte Sauge, 'The Rhetoric of the Interwar Period: The Competition for a New Office Building for the Norwegian Shipowners' Association', in *The Architectural Competition. Research Inquiries and Experiences*, eds Magnus Rönn et al. (Stockholm: Axl Books, 2008), 508–531.

CHAPTER 12

NEW PROPOSALS FOR THE REPRESENTATION AND ASSESSMENT OF COMPETITION PROPOSALS

Tiina Merikoski

Planning competitions are used to harness the talents of several design teams at once in order to investigate possible solutions for a specific challenge, for example, for a site to be developed.[1] These competitions are grounded in the tradition of architectural methods of knowledge production, which means that visual imagery and illustrations are the key mode for transmitting ideas and knowledge.[2]

Proposals to a competition are typically submitted anonymously. The imagery is thus meant to be self-explanatory.[3] Instructions and guidelines for submissions are given in the competition brief; these aim to ensure that the design transmits the necessary knowledge, and to mitigate the challenge of representational differences between the proposals. The imagery is premised to be devoid of interpretation, and that it can communicate the knowledge it contains to an audience in a transparent or disinterested way.[4]

In particular, the linear forms of representation in architectural design, such as technical drawings and blueprints, are considered objective forms of representation. Even so, these images are specifically used by the architectural (and engineering) profession, and therefore are harder to read for those who are not familiar with them. Partly for this reason, other forms of imagery are used when the aim is to communicate with an audience outside the architectural profession. Perspectives, renderings and visualisations that mimic the reality are often easier to comprehend for someone not used to professional imagery. Yet these images are even more problematic, since they represent the kind of visual information that can mislead the viewer. Architectural representation aims to visualise the imagined environment in a way that does not only communicate the knowledge embedded in the design but also aims to create an illusion of the environment to become.

The notion of the disinterestedness of the image has been questioned by many scholars and architectural critics. All (artistic) images hold two realities within them, and 'their suggestive power derives from this [...] tension between the real and the suggested'.[5] Furthermore, the idea of a disinterested image simplifies the understanding of the image, as architects work mainly with visual material.[6] This means that, in addition to being a design professional working in the field of construction, the architect is also a trained and skilful image-maker, constructing the image deliberatively and in consideration of the viewer – whether that is the client or the competition jury. It is this process of 'falsification' that challenges the assumed simplicity and disinterestedness of the image.[7] In a competition, this visual rhetoric is meant to appeal to the intuition and emotions of the jury members, but it makes comparing the proposals complicated.

As part of the research project MATKA,[8] a layering method was used to experiment with and address the challenge of incommensurability in imagery, and in the framework of planning for a case study site, a competition was held. The research interest in terms of the competition was to examine how the requirements of sustainability were translated into the proposals, but it was also to find solutions for evaluating and comparing alternative plans. The project was a collaboration between Aalto University departments of architecture and energy technology, and the Finnish Forest Research Institute (Metla). In addition key stakeholders, such as Kolari municipality and Lapland Hotels (as one of the key developers of the site), were involved as project partners.

Experimenting with the competition

The competition used in the MATKA case study was launched in April 2010. Its main objective was to investigate alternative planning solutions for a new resort community. This was an invited competition, and all five selected design teams submitted proposals.

The case study site was located next to Äkäslompolo village in Ylläs, which is a tourism destination in a remote location in Finnish Lapland. The area is known for the ski slopes on Ylläs fell and the two resort villages on opposite sides of the fell. One of the most challenging tasks of the competition was to fit the required number of square metres of new construction[9] onto the steep slopes of the site. Not only are the northwest slopes challenging to construct, but they are also valuable in terms of nature and landscape. Even so, the amount of new construction was considered justified by the proximity of the tourism services and the ski lifts, and to ensure an economically viable business.

The proposals to the competition were submitted in early autumn 2010. All five proposals were deconstructed by MATKA researchers using the layering method. The key idea of the method was to redraw as vector images the information that was relevant to compare – such as land use, buildings and road connections. These were then layered against each other to get a full and 'undisturbed' understanding of the differences between the five proposals (see Figs 3.6 and 3.7). Moreover, the layers could be studied together with any of the existing features of the site (topography and other land and natural elements, existing trails, built environment, etc), which were also available as vector files.

The redrawn layers ignored the renderings and the visual effects that powered the original competition material, which aimed to persuade and impress the members of the jury. By comparing the results of the layers to the original imagery in the proposals, it became evident how easily the viewer is led by the visual rhetoric of proposals. The layering method also underlined how the imagery dominates over the written material within the practice of architectural competition and evaluation.[10] For example, figures for actual square metres of land use were given and are comparable as such, and yet the imagery led the discussion over how much land was used in the proposed designs.

Based on the comparable results of the layers, the researchers provided an analysis of the proposals for the competition jury to support their decision-making. Overall, the proposals suggested variations of plans that fitted well

Figure 3.6
Land use of the winning proposal (in pink) compared with the other entries.
Top left: 'Kuura' and 'Kudelma'; Top right: 'Kuura' and 'Luppo'; Bottom left: 'Kuura'
and 'Noitarumpu'; and Bottom right: 'Kuura' and 'Ylys'. (Images: Tiina Merikoski)

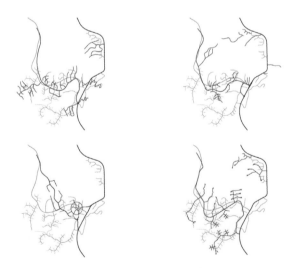

Figure 3.7
Transportation network of the winning proposal (in blue) compared with
the other entries. Top left: 'Kuura' and 'Kudelma'; Top right: 'Kuura' and
'Luppo'; Bottom left: 'Kuura' and 'Noitarumpu'; and Bottom right: 'Kuura'
and 'Ylys'. (Images: Tiina Merikoski)

with the competition guidelines and the existing master plan. Only one out of the five proposals, 'Luppo', suggested a plan with a strong statement for sustainability; it proposed radically less built space than the master plan allowed, leaving as much land free from construction as possible (see Fig. 3.8). However, the proposal was considered unrealistic in terms of the developers' aims for the site, especially since the plan left the highest parts of the site – with the most sensitive nature – unbuilt.

Figure 3.8 Proposal 'Luppo' (courtesy of Aalto University)

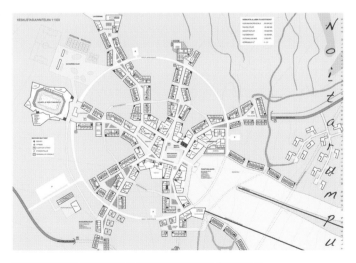

Figure 3.9 Proposal 'Noitarumpu' by Arkkitehtitoimisto Neva Oy gained an honorary mention in the competition (courtesy of Aalto University)

139

Conclusion

The commensurability of the proposals is a challenge in competition assessment. Planning competitions are grounded in the tradition of architectural knowledge production, which means that the imagined future is represented with visual material. In the process of creating an image, architects make decisions on what will be portrayed, what is left out, and how the image is framed. In addition, the chosen methods of illustration combined with the skills of rendering create an illusion of the imagined reality that is meant to win the jury over. The final product is an image which requires high levels of interpretation and imagination, and is not comparable with another image, even if the guidelines for creating that image have been the same for everyone.

What is more, the common formats for submissions – printed panels or digital submission – can only be compared side by side, and not layered against each other. The jury – as with any other viewer of the imagery – easily gets lost in the persuasive world of visualisations, and therefore the knowledge embedded in the images may not be effectively considered.

The layering method tested in the MATKA project aimed to address this challenge of incommensurability. Separating different features of the designs and layering them against each other enabled the viewer to get an undisturbed understanding of the differences between the proposals. The comparisons stepped beyond the chosen visualisation style and techniques. Using this method turned out not to be as laborious as it first seemed. In this study, the chosen features were redrawn in Vectorworks software, but any other CAD software could be used. Nonetheless, somebody still needs to do it. In this case, there were only five proposals to be compared, but in a competition with tens (or even hundreds) of designs, it becomes arduous.

Finally, an interesting question remains: Did the method and its revelations have any effect on the outcome of the competition? In the end, the analysis did give support to choosing the winner. Moreover, it can be noted that the method made comparing the key elements easier, and mitigated the effects of the visual rhetoric. Thus, the method can be used effectively in the assessment of the proposals, and can give support to decision-making, although it should be acknowledged that the aim and purpose of this method is not to become a tool for judging.

Both competition practices and the tradition in architectural knowledge production have come to a point in history where their operational context has changed in a way that no longer supports or justifies commonly used practices. Over the past decades, not only has digitisation brought new and mostly computerised tools for image-making, but the need to respond to environmental challenges has become ever more urgent. Transition towards more sustainable solutions requires an effective, trans-disciplinary collaboration, which also means new methods and tools for design that support co-creation.

The layering method developed in the MATKA project was merely a modest attempt, an experimentation, to mitigate the known challenges of the image in terms of competition evaluation. And as such, it cannot provide all the answers. However, the implications revealed by this experiment add to the pressure to adjust and revise competition practices – also perhaps within the larger scope of architectural knowledge production – according to 21st-century requirements. The tools for image-making are updated and developed continually, and new tools emerge at a fast rate. Thus, it would seem only reasonable to ask for competitors to include new material in their proposals, such as different layers of their design in a specific digital form.

Notes

1   Jonas Andersson, Gerd Bloxham Zettersten and Magnus Rönn eds. *Architectural Competitions: Histories and Practice*, (Hamburg: Rio Kulturkooperativ and Royal Institute of Technology, 2013), 10.

2   See, for example, Andersson et al. (eds.), *Architectural Competitions*; and Tiina Merikoski and Susa Eräranta, 'Intrinsic Mismatches within Architectural Competitions: Case Sibbesborg', in *Nordic Journal of Architectural Research*, No 2, 2015, 41–65.

3   Andersson et al. (eds.), *Architectural Competitions*.

4   Sari Tähtinen, 'Writing Architecture: Textual Image Practices – A Textual Approach in Architectural Research', dissertation, Aalto University, 2013; Hélène Lipstadt, 'Experimenting with the Experimental Tradition, 1989–2009: On Competitions and Architecture Research', in *Nordic Journal of Architectural Research*, Vol 21 No 2/3, 2009, 9–22; Guilherme et al., *Architectural Competitions*.

5   Juhani Pallasmaa, *The Embodied Image: Imagination and Imagery in Architecture* (John Wiley & Sons, 2011), 63.

6   Tähtinen, *Writing Architecture*, 25.

7   Tähtinen, *Writing Architecture*, 61.

8   MATKA was a two-year (2009-2011) research project investigating sustainable solutions for Nordic tourism destinations, and examining the actual planning process of a case study site during this time. The project was based on pragmatic action research methods where the researchers worked together with the project partners that represented the entire value chain of stakeholders of developing the case study site. The name MATKA comes from the complete project's name, Kestävä matkailualue in Finnish, which means a sustainable tourism destination.

9   At the time of the competition the legitimate master plan for Ylläs allowed up to 284,000 m^2 of new construction of hotels, facilities for tourism and commercial services, and another 50,000 m^2 for holiday housing. These numbers were considered as guidelines for the proposals as well.

10 The relationship between the two modes of knowledge production, image and text, in planning competitions has been discussed by, for example, Andersson, Zettersten and Rönn (eds), *Architectural Competitions: Histories and Practice*; Merikoski and Eräranta, 'Intrinsic Mismatches within Architectural Competitions'; Tähtinen, *Writing Architecture*; and Pallasmaa, *The Embodied Image*. Architects use imagery in their work, but many other professionals rely on written material. Yet, in competitions, the role of the text is descriptive. It is meant to support the imagery, and *'to clarify the knowledge that is already deposited in the images'* (Andersson, Zettersten and Rönn, *Architectural Competitions: Histories and Practice*, 10). Thus, the information the text contains remains secondary in its form and content.

EXPERIMENTATION IN CONTEXT

Discussion with Tom Bloxham, Cilly Jansen, Susanna Sirefman and Thomas Hoffmann-Kuhnt

Question (Q): Where does your interest in competitions stem from? How have you been involved in competitions (and what kind of competitions – open/restricted) so far?

Tom Bloxham (TB): We are big advocates of architecture competitions; they are a wonderful way of unearthing new talent in architecture as well as a great way to explore a number of design options. Ultimately, we're big fans of architects, and our developments come from creative processes with great design minds; we're the client whose schemes have won the most RIBA Awards, and that's in part because of the architects with whom we work.

We've carried out lots of architecture competitions over the years, all over the country, and with great success. Notable highlights include the original design competition for our Lister Mills development in Bradford, which was won by David Morley Architects, as well as three separate design competitions at New Islington in Manchester, where Fashion Architecture Taste (FAT) were unanimously selected by the future residents of 23 distinctive houses at Islington Square. Similar competitions in the vicinity saw Mae Architects design houses known as 'The Guts', while 14 further houses were designed by DMFK Architects (formerly de Metz Architects).

One of our best examples of unearthing new talent came back in 2000 when we launched a competition to design a new-build scheme in Castlefield, Manchester – Timber Wharf, now our head office. The winning design for Timber Wharf was from the then little-known Glenn Howells Architects. The building has since won eight awards, including an

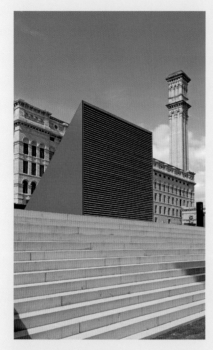

Figures 3.10, 3.11, 3.12 Lister Mills

Figures 3.13, 3.14, 3.15 Timber Wharf

RIBA Award for Architecture – with Glenn also going on to achieve numerous award-winning schemes.

Having completed the 260-home first phase of the Grade II listed Park Hill in Sheffield – a former Stirling

Prize nominee – we launched a competition inviting design practices to create a concept for the second, residential phase of the development. Mikhail Riches was appointed in spring 2016 following a creative six-way pitch. They delivered on a brief to preserve the legacy and efforts of phase-one architect Hawkins\Brown and Studio Egret West, as well as the vision of original architect, Ivor Smith, who designed Park Hill with the late Jack Lynn. Mikhail Riches will now have the job of injecting a fresh aesthetic into the next wave of homes and commercial spaces. A video of the Park Hill competition process can be viewed here: www.youtube.com/watch?v=p_ZYwl3ql1w.

Susanna Sirefman (SS): I am the founder of the leading independent architect selection firm in the US, Dovetail Design Strategists. We specialise in finding the right architect for complex building programmes. Dovetail has crafted and led dozens of competitive

architect selection processes, comprising over half a billion dollars' worth of projects already built or currently in construction. These include international architecture competitions, invited design competitions, RFPs (Request For Proposals), interview-based searches and design concept commissions. Our focus is on cultural, institutional, civic, sacred space and healthcare. Dovetail's clients include the City

Figures 3.16, 3.17 Park Hill

of New York, the Metropolitan Museum of Art, the Cooper Hewitt Smithsonian Design Museum, the Corporation of Yaddo, the New York Public Library and Johns Hopkins University.

Cilly Jansen (CJ): I was educated as an architectural historian and worked as a staff member at the National Foundation for the Arts, Design & Architecture in the 1980s. There I was involved in providing scholarships to young architects and in the decision-making on their applications. That's how I became interested in the selection of architectural plans. But I really became involved in architecture competitions at Architectuur Lokaal, a new national foundation I started in 1993 with the aim of contributing to a meaningful building culture in the Netherlands by improving patronage in architecture. In practice, we initiated projects to professionalise public clients in the commissioning of building projects. We realised that the selection of an architect is a crucial moment in this process, and at the same time, that a competition culture did not really exist in the Netherlands in those days. Municipalities worked with so-called 'architect lists', which made it hard for young architects to enter the market.

In the same year (1993), the first European directives for [architects'] services were adopted. Thus, much discussion arose on European selection procedures between clients and architects, and between architects themselves. So, the chief government architect took the lead in finding solutions, together with architects, housing corporations, project developers, etc. We were invited to join this group, and after a covenant was reached between all parties in 1997, to establish a helpdesk. This became the Steunpunt Architectuuropdrachten & Ontwerpwedstrijden (Architectural Assignments & Design Contests Support Centre). Twenty years later, the Steunpunt is a highly successful system that offers a database covering all notices for public contracts and contests in the field of architecture, assists (public) clients and market operators in the architectural sector, and promulgates best practice. It is a comprehensive system, offering tangible products (digital manuals called Compass, statistics, publications) and intangible services (advice and support). The use of the platform of the Steunpunt is free of charge to all users.

For a few years now, we have cooperated with our UK partner Project Compass in the common portal TheFulcrum.eu, where all announcements of competitions can be found. By increasing the transparency in the market for architecture, and promulgating best practice, we intend to lower entry barriers to public contracts, increase the efficiency and proportionality of public procurement, and stimulate cross-border trade. The Fulcrum focuses on tenders and contests in the Netherlands and the UK. Other countries can join the Fulcrum initiative, provided they are represented by an independent, non-commercial legal entity. We aim to promote a healthy European building culture.

Besides this, I am involved in writing briefs for competitions. Clients make clear what their question is, and we help them formulate a clear procedure. The recognisability of the structure of the briefs – based on a format, but always tailor-made – makes it easier for architects to concentrate on the real question of the competition. Together with my colleagues, I also help public and private parties organise competitions; this concerns mainly open design contests and open development competitions – the latter are open to architects too; it's about the development, *not* about the developers.

Thomas Hoffmann-Kuhnt (THK): What does 'interest' mean in this context? In my case, this word is clearly inadequate – competitions are my life! I have devoted my entire professional life to competitions. As a student of architecture, I realised at the end of the 1960s that there was hardly any information about architectural competitions available, and in 1971 I eventually founded my own publishing company and a monthly magazine, *wa wettbewerbe aktuell* (http://www.wa-journal.

de/de/home.html), which deals exclusively with competitions, and whose main focus until now is the value-neutral documentation of competition results. So, within just under 50 years, a competition archive has been developed that consists of around 6,000 competitions, with well over 30,000 award-winning designs. In addition, there is our digital archive, with a further 10,000 designs, which are not documented in our print edition. I might say that in Germany *wa* is a very important, if not indispensable, tool for all architects who participate in competitions.

Q: With regard to your particular experience, what are competitions' most important plus points and their worst pitfalls when it comes to the implementation of a new building scheme?

THK: Competitions are, without doubt, a truly important element of building culture. Not for nothing are competitions required in Germany for all projects which are publicly subsidised. Of course, there can be mishaps, but usually only when the preparation or implementation is faulty, ie unprofessional. And last but not least, the calls for tender have to be coordinated with the Chamber of Architects.

SS: In my experience, design competitions – in particular design ideas competitions – can be very effective in raising public awareness of a complex design problem, and therefore get the attention of civic decision-makers. Open design ideas competitions cast a broad net, generate publicity, and provide an easily accessible platform for community discourse.

The very first competition I led in 2006 – Urban Voids: Grounds for Change – an international design ideas competition, challenged registrants to present compelling ideas for 40,000 vacant lots in Philadelphia. Conceived as a critical part of a larger campaign to generate ecologically sound and feasible solutions, the competition attracted over 220 entries from 25 countries, including Canada, Chile, Finland, Japan, Korea, New Zealand, Poland, Romania, the United Kingdom and Uruguay. This was the first North American design ideas competition to address the pressing issue of urban vacancy, and Urban Voids provided multiple visions for government agencies and communities around the country to explore and implement in their own backyards.

The worst pitfall for open design competitions, and a personal pet peeve, is open design ideas competitions, framed as open design competitions, where the competition sponsor does not have the resources, or even worse, has no intention of building the project. We have observed that in the US and abroad, the open design competition format is sometimes misused as a political

tool to gauge public buy-in for a project, without a true commitment to building the solution – wasting competitors' time and resources.

CJ: I firmly believe that consistency and continuity for 20 years have been very important in developing a modern and transparent competition culture in the Netherlands. And that the independence of Architectuur Lokaal is indispensable for all parties involved. Besides, a system of 'self-certification' proved to be interesting. This resulted from the way in which we developed the formats – together with all stakeholders, so that the procedures were widely endorsed. One of the biggest problems was the workload for architects, which could be called disproportional.

TB: We believe that when we have a competition we should be picking a team and not a scheme – it's about finding partners who inspire us with their thinking, and inevitably a competition-winning scheme evolves.

Q: What do clients/stakeholders look for when organising a competition? Are there situations where competitions are avoided?

CJ: [Clients/stakeholders are looking] for new ways of working, because problems may not be easily defined nowadays; there are no known or prescribed solutions. Furthermore, the results of consultations with the public bring uncertainty. The traditional linear organisation of construction projects – starting with the clients (possibly public authorities), passing through the architects, and consultation with users – has completely altered. Clients are therefore looking for new solutions to new problems.

THK: Competitions offer the unique opportunity to select the best designs for the project from a large number of submitted entries. This is appreciated not only by public clients, but also by private clients. From personal experience, I can say that there is no rational reason to advise against a competition procedure – from a single-family home to various large-scale projects, [though] always according to the premise of a transparent and fair procedure.

SS: Because the United States has no regulatory requirements governing the architect selection process, there are many options by which to choose an architect.

At Dovetail, we are very clear about the difference between choosing a design or a designer. In a design competition, selection is based on a project-specific design proposal. In other competitive selection processes, the designer (architect or design team) is selected based on their design approach as evidenced in prior work, methodology and philosophy.

Client and stakeholder goals for the architect selection process should be the determining factors in crafting the appropriate structure for architect procurement. Is the client interested in seeing multiple potential solutions to a complex problem? Then a design competition may make sense. How broad a range of stakeholders exists in the project? Is visibility for a future project perceived as a positive or negative? Most importantly, prior to deciding to run a design competition, it must be clear that a client has the appropriate resources to spend on commissioning design concepts.

Trained as an architect myself, I am a passionate advocate for architects, believing that design competitions should be avoided if a client does not have the budget for (or is not willing to spend appropriately on) concept design.

TB: Our approach to competitions is fairly open as we are fearful of restrictions that impede the creativity of the process; sometimes we have blind competitions, sometimes we have open competitions, sometimes we have invited competitions with just a handful of architects – and sometimes we have competitions of just one.

Q: Do you think that certain competition types are preferable for specific building programmes? What should the applied criteria be when choosing the type of competition to be organised?

SS: The desired outcome for a project (as well as the goals and objectives for the selection process itself) is the key to determining what format a competitive selection process should be – not the building programme.

THK: We basically have three types of competitions in Germany. The open competition allows any architect to participate; the so-called limited open competition allows each architect to apply for the participation, but the client can select a previously determined number of participants from the entries according to pre-defined criteria. And the third type is the well-known invitation competition, with its various variations: two-stage or the combination of invitation and open or limited open competition. In the case of limited open competitions – the most common competition type in Germany – usually the experience of planning a comparable project is required; this is understandable for projects such as laboratory construction. However, the selection of such criteria leads ultimately to a small circle of specialists, which in my opinion is not desirable. Still, I always recommend open competitions, because they usually achieve the most promising results.

TB: It is important to get an experienced jury and ensure that they can properly interpret drawings and aren't seduced by beautiful images that are impossible to engineer or build to a budget. Competitions can also be a good methodology for raising the profile of a project, and by including other parties, community groups, English Heritage, or local politicians on the jury, it's a way of bringing stakeholders into the project. Competitions have been announced through statutory journals like OJEU, but we've also found a positive experience partnering with architectural publications.

If practices are inexperienced and want to enter competitions, it's always reassuring as a client to see smaller, younger practices partnering with other larger, experienced consultants, like engineers and quantity surveyor firms.

Q: How do you think the notion of experimentation may be interpreted in terms of the production of the built environment? What about the notion of innovation? How may experimentation or innovation be understood in the context of architectural competitions, and from a client's point of view?

THK: This is exactly the decisive advantage of competitions; here one can finally dare to do something! Depending on the knowledge about the composition of the jury and their preferences, you could even say that you should absolutely do something! Because competitions offer the best conditions for innovative designs and experimental construction. Just think of Zaha Hadid, Coop Himmelb(l)au or Daniel Libeskind, to name but a few. They all started as 'no names', received their first contracts based on winning competitions in Germany, and established their international reputation through competition successes. So, it is not a question of competitions being the key for innovation and experiment, it is rather the question of whether the client is willing to engage him or herself, and to risk experiment.

SS: Innovation always costs more in the short term than maintaining the status quo. A client must have a clear understanding of this, have the capability and willingness to invest in innovation, and be able to envision the ultimate big picture, long-term cost savings and rewards of an experimental project. This is a big issue in the United States, where the value of design excellence and design innovation has not been widely embraced.

TB: Experimentation and innovation went hand in hand on our most recent design competition for the second phase of Park Hill in Sheffield. The complex fabric of the building meant that it was imperative that shortlisted practices were given a space in the building in which they could experiment, ensuring their designs were suitable for the concrete structure. Each practice had two weeks to design 'their' apartment as they wished, before then 'inviting' Urban Splash and our

partners in for a look around – it was such a refreshing way of doing things, and really stimulating to see the variety of ways each practice chose to describe their vision.

Q: What is your opinion of competition architecture?

TB: We're big fans: competitions have really helped us with the creative process, and although we adapt and evolve our competitions, they remain an interesting part of our design and development process.

SS: Meaningful competition architecture needs to represent a big idea – an idea that speaks to the larger context of a project, and that will survive multiple iterations of the design.

THK: Allow me to ask a counter-question: What does competition architecture mean? Because I don't think there is a generally valid definition, I would like to emphasise the following: competitions not only offer the best conditions for the most suitable and ideal design for a project but they also allow the client the chance to implement a real highlight of architecture. Just think of the Eiffel Tower in Paris, the Houses of Parliament in London, The White House in Washington – monument-protected competition projects, by which these cities are nowadays identified. Competitions are often the prerequisite for milestones of building culture. But this does

152

not only imply a brilliant design by an architect, but also a jury that recognises the genius of a design, and a client who has the courage to implement it!

Q: In your view, what kinds of competitions profit from extensive visibility in the press? How is press coverage important for competitions and the building schemes related to them?

SS: In 2013, in response to the devastation of Hurricane Sandy, and in keeping with then Mayor Bloomberg's resiliency mandate, Dovetail was engaged by well-known actress Bette Midler's not-for-profit New York Restoration Project to develop and lead a design competition for a state-of-the-art, flood-resistant outdoor recreation and learning centre along the Harlem River in Manhattan, New York. We recommended an invited design competition, seeking multidisciplinary teams headed up by young, emerging architects. The competition – EDGE|ucation Pavilion Design Competition – and Dovetail-organised accompanying exhibition (featuring the design of the winning firm, Bade Stageberg Cox Architects, and all eight competitor schemes) garnered so much attention that a prominent philanthropist approached New York Restoration Project and asked to fund the project. This is an excellent example of the right match of selection process format and client. Visibility from a design

competition can be instrumental for institutions that are growing, want to raise their profile, and demonstrate an investment in both design excellence and their community.

THK: The publication of competitions in any form is, in my opinion, extremely important, which is why I founded the magazine *wa* and the competition archive. Because – and this was, after all, the most illuminating insight, and at the same time the catalyst of my entire professional life – only through documentation and publication of the winning designs (not just the first prize) are competitions made known to the wider public, and furthermore, jury decisions become comprehensible! Also, and this is fundamental for a retrospective consideration, a specific zeitgeist can be detected, and a trend can be demonstrated. Apart from this, it has also been shown that it is important to involve the public at an early stage in the process of a project. Thus, lengthy public petitions can be avoided that can delay or even question the implementation of the project.

TB: We have in the past experimented with competitions in conjunction with media partners such as *AJ* and *BD* magazines. We've found it's a great way of amplifying the existence of the competition and broadening our reach. As the media has evolved, we've also found a lot of success in word of mouth via social media platforms – again, this has been beneficial in ensuring more architects hear about the competition and want to get involved.

Q: How are new competitions announced? How can architects and all interested parties keep track of them?

SS: Our open design competitions are typically announced digitally through major media outlets and a variety of social media platforms. Dovetail design competition announcements quickly go viral, and attract hundreds of entries from around the globe.

THK: All competitions, not just the German ones, are announced by a European central office in Brussels, to which we have direct access, so that we can inform our readers about the latest competitions with a daily updated newsletter. We also report in our monthly magazine about the further course of the competition, about the results, who received the contract, up to the completed project.

TB: Online through the Urban Splash website as well as through partner channels and social media.

Q: Could you describe a competition procedure that you consider exemplary, and elaborate on your reasons for thinking so?

THK: Our archive comprises approximately 6,000 competitions, and I could give you numerous

examples. From this experience let me state in general terms that the success of a competition depends on at least three factors. First, a sound, professionally prepared call for tender must be guaranteed as a prerequisite. The second, but unpredictable, factor is the participants, with their wealth of innovative ideas. However, [the level of this unpredictability] is influenced by the type of competition, eg an open competition with invitation, and is thus quite controllable. The third factor is a competent jury, which has to recognise the quality of the entries. As they say, a competition result can only be as good as the jury.

SS: At Dovetail we have developed a very successful proprietary selection process that works extremely well for the architects invited to participate, for our clients and for the diverse, external stakeholders typically involved in large, complex projects. This is a competitive process that identifies the right design team, rather than a right design.

Dovetail recently led the New York Public Library (NYPL) through our process for their $300m renovation and re-imagination of their 5th Avenue flagship research library, the Stephen A. Schwarzman Building, in conjunction with NYPL's largest circulating library, the Mid-Manhattan Library, directly across the street. Our three-phase invited selection process, for which Dovetail created a stellar shortlist, included a Request for

Qualifications (RFQ), a Request for Proposals (RFP), a written response to a Request for Information (RFI), office visits, existing project site visits and finalist interviews. Mecanoo, whose headquarters are in the Netherlands, teamed up with the New York-based firm Beyer Blinder Belle as architect-of-record, won the commission, and work is well underway.

The greatest benefit to our process is that it allows for extensive structured dialogue between the competitors and potential future client. This, in turn, ensures that all parties are clear on the project brief, the expectations for decision-making and project goals.

CJ: At Architectuur Lokaal, together with the stakeholders, we have found a solution for the disproportional workload of architects within the context of competitions: a competition procedure in two rounds, in which the vision of the entries leads, is increasingly used. The designers (and their partners, since participation in multidisciplinary teams becomes the standard) are asked to give their vision on innovation, with reference images, *but without a design*. The designers of the best visions are invited to make a design, based on their selected vision, for the second round, and they are compensated for their work. Good examples are the open competitions for the World Heritage Centre in Kinderdijk and the Prins Clausbrug [a bridge] in

Dordrecht. For both procedures, the briefs were written in the Compass formats, and the procedures were in two rounds. In both [competitions] there were about 130 entries in the first round. Five were selected for the second round, and they received compensation for their work; the public were involved, etc. The procedures were in accordance with European legislation. There have been no problems at all, and most importantly, the selected architects would not have been eligible for these commissions if it had involved tenders instead of competitions. Both winning plans are currently under construction.

TB: We've learned something new from each of our competitions, and have applied that thinking to ensure subsequent architectural processes are evolved and improved. The aforementioned competition to design phase two of Park Hill in Sheffield is perhaps the most prominent in our minds. Playing on the broader marketing campaign for the development, we invited architects to pitch with a fun and enticing brief in the form of a marriage proposal! Fifteen practices responded, and the six who were shortlisted were sent a second-stage brief announcing that we were 'engaged'. It was a fun way of using a successful broader hook, and meant the brief appealed to lots of practices.

Other competition processes of ours have been documented by RIBA, including:

Timber Wharf www.architecture.com/RIBA/Competitions/CaseStudies/Housing/TimberWharf/TimberWharf.aspx.

Islington Square: www.architecture.com/RIBA/Competitions/CaseStudies/Housing/IslingtonSquare/IslingtonSquare.aspx.

Q: What advice would you give, as a competition organiser/stakeholder/consultant/juror/press representative, with respect to competitions and participating in them to architects only just entering the professional arena?

SS: For architects, the decision to participate in a design competition should be treated as a business decision. For example, an invited process – whether a design competition or RFQ – statistically increases the odds for a firm to win, making it a less risky proposition.

Due diligence on the competition sponsors and organisers should be undertaken prior to entering, and should include exploring the following questions: Does the proposed project have funding already in place? Is it likely to get built or is the goal of the competition simply to raise awareness of a potential future project? Does this matter to your firm? Do you

have the time and resources to devote to a speculative project? Is the compensation offered by the competition (financial or marketing) appropriate for the work requested? Does the competition offer an intellectual stimulant for your office? This is often a valuable trade-off for young firms whose bread and butter projects might not be as sexy as the competition subject. Who are the jurors? Are they meaningful stakeholders in the project, capable of pushing the project forward, or is a star-studded jury constituted to fulfil the organiser's (not the client's) agenda?

THK: As the success story of all great 'star architects' has taught us, I can only give the advice to participate in as many competitions as possible. Architects have certainly internalised this, because there is no other professional group that invests so much time, work and money in competitions, even though they know that there can be only one winner. Architects entering the professional arena should always encourage themselves [to participate], and spare no effort and money, if possible even while they are still a student. This is why we have also organised the annual *wa* award for students, which is very popular in German-speaking universities. Generally speaking, the key to success in competitions is not only elaborate plans and perfect renderings but also exciting ideas, and/or the courage to present them. This is the only way to win. And then there is not only one winner, but the client (and ideally society) are winners as well, and everyone will be happy!

TB: The best advice would be that, no matter how small a practice a new architect feels they are, still enter these competitions; they are a great way of getting work noticed by developers. From Glenn Howells to FAT, we've discovered some incredible architects via our competitions, who've now gone on to be global design players. I would tell new architects not to be scared or let anything stop them putting their creativity out there.

CJ: My advice to inexperienced architects would be: read the brief well, try to understand what the client is looking for, use the opportunity to ask questions, and don't enter unreasonable procedures. Employ common sense.

PART 4

REVISITING ARCHITECTURAL
COMPETITIONS' STRUCTURES AND FORMS

CHAPTER 14

COMPETITIVE STRAIN SYNDROME

Jeremy Till

In the introduction to one of the few books that addresses the contemporary architectural competition, the authors write: 'Every competition remains a world of possibilities: an intermediary space–time locus for the search for excellence in architecture. In some ways, competition projects *function like utopias*.'[1] This essay examines the claim that competitions represent a form of utopia. It argues that, while at face value they present an image of creative experiment and formal freedom, they do so on the back of an apparatus that can be read as deeply exploitative. Competitions are heralded as delivering architectural advances, but these so-called innovations mask an unattractive underlying system.

False utopias

One of the most acute analyses of utopias is that of David Harvey, who identifies two prevalent forms of utopias.[2] First, utopias of social process, which propose new forms of social organisation. Second, utopias of spatial form, which are based on new formal solutions. Harvey notes that, taken separately, the two forms of utopias are flawed. Those of social processes are generally developed without a spatial context; 'they are literally bound to no place whatsoever.'[3] Those of spatial form are described out of temporal and social context, and so 'get perverted from their noble objectives by having to compromise with the social processes they are meant to control'.[4] It is the latter type of utopia that is aspired to in the architectural competition in its presentation of static, perfected forms lifted out of time, and out of the social processes that both produced them and will eventually occupy them.

The apparent freedom that the competition delivers is one of its attractions to architects, and of course has historically delivered examples of formal and stylistic innovation. The seminal competition-winning schemes – Sydney Opera House, Pompidou Centre, Parc de la Villete and so on – are often used as justification for the competition system on the grounds that such breakthroughs would not have happened under normal procurement methods, fettered as they are by numerous controls. In their utopias of spatial form, architectural competitions are a last refuge, where architects can play out their intimate association with the object. Architects feel that they are in complete control for that fleeting moment of the production of the competition entry, away from the dependencies and demands of others. As the authority and control of the architect has decreased in the contemporary production systems of the built environment, the competition becomes an ever more attractive sanctuary for the exercise of architectural aspirations and experiment.

The privileging of the architectural object in the architectural competition is an inevitability of a system that relies on drawings as the primary mode of representation and evaluation. As Hélène Lipstadt notes, the competition is 'a procedure that considers ... the drawing to be an adequate prefiguration of the desired building, capable of being compared with other similar ones and judged for its aesthetic superiority'.[5] Lipstadt identifies that the birth of the architectural competition in 14th-century Renaissance Italy was dependent on the birth of the architectural drawing as a particular form of expertise that distinguished the architect from the builder or artist. She further argues that:

> *'The competitions of the Renaissance, and the status that they bestowed upon architects, inform the mythology that still pervades the contemporary process ... The gift of the Renaissance competition and its historiography is that of autonomy, the patent of architecture's nobility. Because the competition project is conceived in the autonomy of a relation of designer to program and not in the give-and-take of exchange with the client, it is the preeminent example of architectural creation that is at once autonomous and socially legitimated as part of practice.'[6]*

The feeling of autonomy provided by the competition brings with it a sense of authority and control for the architect, but this comes with some serious limitations. Most obviously, by foregrounding architectural representation, the competition frames the discussion of architecture in aesthetic and formal terms, and in this presents architecture as a timeless entity beyond the reach of social processes.

The competition creates what Malcolm Reading – one of the main promoters of architectural competitions – calls a 'partial vacuum,'[7] into which the client is sucked in order to contribute their take on taste and function. Anyone who has sat on either side of a competition jury process can bear witness to how taste is always circling round the table, often in an unspoken (but still powerful) manner. This has always been the case, from the 18th- and 19th-century academicians of France and Italy using competitions as an 'important part of their practice of criticism, theorisation and tastemaking'[8] to the Victorian era in the United Kingdom, where architects, as self-defined 'men of taste',[9] exercised their aesthetic authority in the adjudication of competitions.

This concentration on aesthetics, function and form in the competition process means that other concerns are suppressed, most notably the life of the building as it unfolds over time. The Dutch architect JP Oud was clear about this in his criticism of competitions: 'It is precisely the incessant to-and-fro between the wishes of the sponsor and the ideas of the architect which make building into a living embodiment of society's needs. It is in this respect that competitions are hopelessly inadequate; because of this permanent lack of contact they lead to a cut-out architecture ... because the contact between life and design is so minimal in competitions it is best to use them sparingly.'[10]

The client's role is reduced to contributing to the brief, and then sometimes attending interviews, where they can make impulsive value judgments as to whether they will 'get on' with the architect. Any sense of spatial production being a process of co-design over time is therefore lost, and with it the full social engagement with the project. In this light it is hard to agree with RIBA's recent assertion that competitions are 'a highly successful procurement model that brings out the best in a project',[11] unless one judges success within the limited purview of taste and refinement. In addition to reducing the engagement with the client to the bare minimum, it is hard to understand how a process that involves only cursory (if any) engagement with the physical and social context could deliver the best results.

If, therefore, the competition operates as any form of utopia, it must be seen as providing false hopes of excellence. But the fixation on the object beautiful also distracts from much more serious issues, namely the exploitative processes that underlie the production within the competitive process.

Vampires of the profession

'Every competition, if at all extensive, costs the profession hundreds of thousands of dollars, most of which falls on men who can ill afford the loss ... No wonder that the system (of competitions) has come to be regarded as a sort of nightmare, as an incubus or vampire, stifling the breath of professional life, and draining its blood.'[12]

The close identification of architecture with its objects is not particular to the competition system: it is a characteristic of the wider discipline. The popular understanding of what architects do is that they design buildings. This much is true, but they also do a lot more than that. They use multiple modes of knowledge in that spatial production – technical, social, visual, processual, historical, cultural and so on. But what architectural culture validates through its education, media and awards is the final object of production. Academic validation boards (in the UK at least) obsess over pictures of buildings in student portfolios. Internet sites are saturated with images of empty sunlit buildings. Awards systems are too often judged on the basis of a flick-through portfolio of such images.

The production of competition drawings in a partial vacuum, removed from the cut and thrust of actual practice, allows architects to believe the myth of pure experimentation as a contribution to cultural and architectural innovation. The production of pure objects in the competition system presumes to detach architecture from the marketplace, a connection that the profession has always found problematic because it compromises the ideal of architect as artist. The competition thus exaggerates a condition that Peggy Deamer has identified as operating through the profession, namely a belief that architects are 'outside of the work/labor discourse because what they do (is) art or design rather than work per se'.[13]

But of course, participating in a competition is a form of labour, and it is important to acknowledge it as such. In delivering such labour for little or no financial reward, the profession allows itself to be exploited. Worse, it abandons the idea that architectural knowledge has monetary value. The architectural competition perpetuates 'the disastrous idea that our value resides in the object we produce and not in the knowledge that produced it'.[14] Competitions can therefore be read as a form of self-sacrifice, both economically and epistemologically. This sacrifice is captured in Louis Kahn's identification of a competition as 'an offering to architecture',[15] although I suspect that he meant this offering was a noble act rather than a gift of labour.

It is extraordinary that the profession not only allows this sacrifice to happen but also actually arranges for it.

RIBA is proud of the competition service that it provides to clients, upholding the quality that the system produces as the primary justification. In its guidance to clients, RIBA notes: 'Competitions enable a wide variety of approaches to be explored simultaneously with a number of designers.'[16] This statement, delivered with no apparent doubt, confirms that competitions are a means of extracting free or extremely cheap labour and knowledge from the profession, an abandonment overseen and sanctioned by the professional institute. One might note that, if the client had clearer views of their project, a wide variety of approaches would not be necessary; and if a wide variety is delivered, then it is legitimate to question against what criteria they can possibly be evaluated. Instead, the competition is presented as a fishing expedition, with architects doing handstands in order to catch the jury's eye – 'gymnasts in the prison yard' indeed.[17]

RIBA is also apparently willing to give up its members' time and knowledge to suit the wider aims of a competition project. With its list of benefits of a competition including to 'raise a project's profile', it is clear that some clients use competitions as a form of public relations in order to present the project in a better light, with credibility given by the engagement of multiple architects. This happened most notoriously in the Helsinki Guggenheim competition organised by Malcolm Reading Consultants, launched in 2014 without confirmed funding. Some 1,751 entries and two years later, the project was abandoned when Helsinki City Council voted against funding it. If one takes a very low estimate of £5,000 worth of labour for each entry, then this represents over £8.5m of lost labour, approximately 10% of the overall project cost.[18] It is worth quoting Malcolm Reading's comments on the abandonment in full, because they say so much about what is wrong with the culture and processes of competitions.

> *'2016 has turned out to be a year of extraordinary events and turmoil and perhaps the final vote should be seen from this perspective. The proposition for a Guggenheim in Helsinki captured the imagination of the global architectural community and the competition was a phenomenon in its own right. One of the most entered design contests in history with entries from 77 countries, it recorded a moment in the architectural zeitgeist. The website is a fantastic resource for architects and architectural enthusiasts and it has recorded just short of 4.5 million page views. We feel for the competitors and finalists but nothing is entirely lost. The intensity of designing to such a compelling brief generates ideas and viewpoints that continue to be explored in subsequent work.'[19]*

First, Reading disingenuously associates the abandonment of the competition with the political events of 2016 – Brexit and Trump. Second, he makes the oft-repeated argument that the larger the number of entries, the greater the success of the competition, when if viewed through the frame of labour, the opposite is the case. Third, he presents the website as a repository of architectural knowledge. The primary knowledge available is that of stylistic comparison, in a snapshot of contemporary forms. Real architectural knowledge, in terms of the embedded and external intelligence that it took to develop each entry, is only superficially accessible given the paucity of the evidence presented for it. As Deamer notes, 'the myth here is that a project assigned to four A1 boards and 500 words offers either the designer or the "community" deep thinking on either site or program'.[20] Finally, Reading suggests that the very act of entering a competition is a way of developing an architect's skills and approaches for future work. This is sometimes used by architects as justification for entering competitions, but only really achieved when that developmental aim is clearly set aside from any dreams of actually winning. It is those dreams that dominate the competition mentality, and the collapse of them for all but a handful of entries builds the disappointment and resentment of an entire profession.

It may be argued that the Helsinki Guggenheim, in all its extremes, does not represent the competition system as a whole. However, in terms of sacrificed labour and knowledge, its problems can be identified to a greater or lesser extent across the range of competitions. At the better end of the scale, invited competitions have become the norm for some architects to obtain work. Over time, these architects – who are generally at the elite end of the profession – can calculate their success rate and the cost of entry, and build this into their business model.[21] But all this comes at real economic loss to the profession, a loss that is too often mitigated by the enforcement of excessive working hours and/or unpaid internships as the only way of getting competition entries completed. At the other end of the scale from the elite invited competitions are the open, and sometimes unregulated, competitions, which typically attract hundreds of entries from younger hopefuls. These competitions are not only financially exploitative but also prey on the aspirations of the profession. Such is the will to create, such is the desperation to succeed, that architects (apparently willingly) sacrifice themselves to the competition machine, vampirish though it is to the profession.

The breakthrough of a single architect in a competition is made on the back of hundreds of other sacrifices, accompanied by endless frustration. This condition is typical of what Guy Standing has termed 'the precariat', a wide class of people who live out their employment in a state of precariousness, both financial and emotional. The precariat are 'people with a relatively high level of formal education who have to accept jobs that have a status or income beneath what they believe accord with their qualifications, are likely to suffer status frustration'.[22] To liken architects to Uber drivers or graphic designers who submit free work to logo mills might appear hyperbolic, but this combination of low pay, frustration and jeopardy is exactly what is induced by the competition system. If one adds to this economic precarity the 'complete drain on intelligence'[23] that Rem Koolhaas identifies in competitions, then it is surely time to question the system as it presently stands.

A spatio–temporal approach

Clearly, architectural competitions are not going to be abandoned completely; but they surely can be adjusted in their processes. The clue to a revised approach may lie in David Harvey's reformulation as necessarily combining the temporal and the spatial, so bringing the social to the formal, and the dynamic to the static.[24] A certain set of implications flow from this.

First, all competitions need to be seen only as the start of the process, not as the end. Too often the winning scheme is considered as a fait accompli, with the client later only tweaking bits within the formal envelope. Competitions should never be seen as providing design 'solutions'; how could they be, given such cursory engagement with the real dynamics of site and social context? Instead, they should be taken as the beginnings of a conversation; table settings which will be necessarily disturbed over the course of the later co-design process.

Second, competitions should have clear filters in place to limit economic (and with it social) loss on the part of the profession. This can be achieved through limiting the numbers of entries. Numbers of entries need to be restricted, either by strict two-stage filters or a sortition process (which randomly selects a fixed number of entries that meet baseline criteria).[25] People may argue that this restriction will simultaneously stifle the aspirations of those excluded, but surely it is better to enter fewer competitions with greater chance of success than it is to enter more with less chance?

Third, the criteria by which competitions are assessed need to revised to take in the spatio–temporal aspects of architecture, and not just the aesthetic and formal ones. There is an increasing expectation for architects to present 'complete' buildings as part of the competition process, an expectation aided by the computer's presumed ability to summon up reality from unreal elements. This expectation needs to be challenged for what it is: a complete waste of the multiple modes of architectural knowledge, and also a form of fake completeness. Instead, we need to shift from an emphasis on visual evidence to other forms of spatio–temporal descriptions.

Maybe the next large architectural competition should be to redesign the architectural competition, using the above observations as a starter, but filling out the conversation with many more.

Notes

1 *Competitions and the Production of Culture, Quality and Knowledge: An International Inquiry*, eds Jean-Pierre Chupin, Carmela Cucuzzella and Bechara Helal (Montreal: Potential Architecture Books, 2015), 12.

2 David Harvey, *Spaces of Hope* (Edinburgh: Edinburgh University Press, 2000), 173ff.

3 *Ibid*, 174.

4 *Ibid*, 179.

5 Hélène Lipstadt, 'The Experimental Tradition', in *The Experimental Tradition: Essays on Competitions in Architecture*, ed. Hélène Lipstadt (New York: Princeton Architectural Press, 1989), 13.

6 *Ibid*, 15.

7 Malcolm Reading, 'How Deep Thinking Wins Competitions', *Architects' Journal*, 24 April 2015. http://www.architectsjournal.co.uk/news/business/how-deep-thinking-wins-competitions/8681626. article. The full quote reads: 'Running a competition is a particular kind of accelerated design activity. Like a journey in space, everything moves at intense speed but is conducted in a partial vacuum. Some architects criticise this absence of the client voice in competitions, but this attitude is unnecessarily sophistic, and the good architect sees an opportunity to fill the gap with content.' As will become apparent, I think criticism of the lack of client voice is far from sophistry.

8 Barry Bergdoll, 'Competing in the Academy and the Marketplace: European Architecture Competitions 1401–1927', in *The Experimental Tradition: Essays on Competitions in Architecture*, ed. Hélène Lipstadt (New York: Princeton Architectural Press, 1989), 25–26.

9 At the first meeting of RIBA in 1835, the secretary of the proposed new organisation called on architects 'to uphold in *ourselves* the character of Architects, as *men* of taste, men of science, men of honour.' Thomas Donaldson, 'Report of the Proceedings, at the Opening General Meeting of the Members' (London: RIBA, 1835). (My emphasis.)

10 As quoted in Hilde de Haan and Ids Haagsma, *Architects in Competition: International Architectural Competitions of the Last 200 Years* (London: Thames and Hudson, 1988), 18.

11 RIBA, *Design Competitions Guidance for Clients* (London: RIBA, 2012), 2. http:www.//competitions. architecture.com/Doc/Guidance_For_Clients.pdf.

12 As quoted in Lipstadt, 'The Experimental Tradition', 15.

13 Peggy Deamer, *The Architect as Worker: Immaterial Labor, the Creative Class, and the Politics of Design*, ed. Peggy Deamer (Bloomsbury Academic, 2015, xxx).

14 Peggy Deamer, 'Work', in *The Architect as Worker*, 72.

15 As quoted in Lipstadt, 'The Experimental Tradition', 10.

16 *Design Competitions Guidance for Clients*, 5.

17 This follows Tafuri. 'How ineffectual are the brilliant gymnastics carried out in the yard of the model prison, in which architects are left free to move about on temporary reprieve.' Manfredo Tafuri, *Theories and History of Architecture* (London: Granada, 1980), xxii. See also chapter 11 of Jeremy Till, *Architecture Depends* (Cambridge: MIT Press, 2009).

18 Peggy Deamer estimates an overall loss of $6,860,000, on the basis of 80 hours per entry. Either way, the value of lost labour is considerable. Peggy Deamer, 'The Guggenheim Helsinki Competition: What Is the Value Proposition?'. http:www.//averyreview.com.

19 Merlin Fulcer, "Guggenheim Helsinki scrapped after city councillors refuse funding". https://www.architectsjournal.co.uk/news/guggenheim-helsinki-scrapped-after-city-councillors-refuse-funding/10015368. article?search=https%3a%2f%2fwww.architectsjournal.

20 *Ibid*.

21 A comparative table in Judith Strong's book on competitions shows how many competitions some elite firms have entered, and their success rate: Foster + Partners, 48 competitions entered in past five years, success rate 19%; Richard Rogers Partnership, 47, 38%; Future Systems, 12 (five UK), 17%; Cullinan Studio, 11, 36%; Matthew Priestman, 12, 17%. Judith Strong, *Winning by Design: Architectural Competitions* (Oxford: Butterworth-Heinemann, 1996), 79. The success rate for open competitions is clearly much lower.

22 Guy Standing, *The Precariat: The New Dangerous Class* (London: Bloomsbury Academic, 2011), 10.

23 Rem Koolhaas, 'There's Been Very Little Rethinking Of What Cities Can Be', 20 March 2015. Http://www.Fastcodesign.Com/3044008/rem-koolhaas-theres-been-very-little-rethinking-of-what-cities-can-be. The full quote is 'there is an incredible amount of wasted effort in the profession. A fair amount of it is generated through the procedure of competitions, which is a complete drain of intelligence. I don't know of any other profession that would tolerate this. At the same time you are important, we invite your thinking, but we also announce that there is an eighty per cent chance that we will throw away your thinking and make sure that it is completely wasted.'

24 'The task then is to define an alternative, not in terms of some static spatial form or even of some perfected emancipatory process. The task is to pull together a spatiotemporal utopianism – a dialectical utopianism – that is rooted in our present possibilities at the same time as it points towards different trajectories.' Harvey, *Spaces of Hope*, 182.

25 For sortition in competitions see Walter Menteth et al., *Design Contest Guidance* (London: Project Compass, 2015), 40.

CHAPTER 15

DESIGNING THE HIGH LINE: DEFINING THE HIGH LINE THROUGH DESIGN COMPETITIONS

Robert Hammond

Since opening in 2009, the High Line has become an integral part of New York's landscape, visited by nearly 8 million people annually. What most people don't realise is that the High Line's transformation was an unlikely story, and that a public design competition played a huge role in propelling the project forward. Stretching over a mile and a half through several iconic New York neighbourhoods – from the West Village, through the Meatpacking district and West Chelsea, and terminating at 34th Street, just below the Jacob K. Javits Convention Center – what was once an abandoned elevated rail is now a continuous greenway that is maintained, operated and programmed by the non-profit conservancy Friends of the High Line (FHL), in partnership with the NYC Department of Parks and Recreation.

Prior to its transformation, the High Line was known to many people by what could be seen from ground level: a rusting steel structure floating above the streets of Manhattan's West Side. It was a relic from New York's industrial past. Once trains stopped running on the structure, a wild landscape took root in the ballast of the tracks, creating a ribbon of green cutting through the cityscape. Architects and designers used the High Line as a site for hundreds of design charrettes and propositions. The most well-known proposal was Steven Holl's 'Bridge of Houses' project in 1981, which proposed repurposing the High Line by building housing and public space on the unused structure.

Design competitions played a pivotal role in the development of the High Line. The competitions brought together the design community – including artists, planners, architects and landscape architects – to help start a dialogue about the importance of civic engagement and the role of design in rethinking disused infrastructure.

Friends of the High Line

FHL was co-founded in 1999 by Joshua David and Robert Hammond, two local residents with no prior experience in design and planning. They dedicated their early grassroots efforts to advocate for the High Line's preservation and reuse as a public space.

At that time, the project seemed nearly impossible because of various political, financial and legal hurdles: there was a lawsuit in place between FHL and the City of New York trying to reverse the demolition order that Mayor Rudolph Giuliani had signed before leaving office; FHL had raised little money to help support their advocacy efforts, and there was not a direct path to ownership of the structure, as the High Line was seen as a liability to CSX, the structure's owner. Many in the neighbourhood viewed the High Line as an eyesore, and the project raised concerns from residents and property owners who could not imagine how the project could be repurposed or become an asset for the community.

FHL recognised that leveraging the design community was one of the simplest ways of bringing attention to the project. Because the organisation's founders did not possess a design background, there was no prescribed design vision being imposed on the project. The idea of organising competitions played a pivotal role in the High Line's transformation, by creating momentum for the project, initiating a dialogue about the High Line's future, creating interest in (and awareness of) the project at a time when many had never even heard of it.

Designing the High Line – 2003 ideas competition

In 2003, the first of two competitions for the High Line was organised. This first iteration was an open, international ideas competition aimed at soliciting innovative proposals for the structure's reuse. Because it was presented as an ideas competition, entries did not have to be practical or realistic, nor did they have to be submitted by design professionals. Entrants were encouraged to be bold and forward-thinking, and to create visions as unique and unexpected as the High Line itself.

At that time, FHL was small, and unfamiliar with how to organise a competition. FHL contacted the Van Alen Institute, a non-profit organisation that focuses on promoting civic projects by organising design competitions. The Van Alen Institute turned down the request, saying that they felt the project was 'too unrealistic'. And they were not the only ones: the project was still viewed as so unlikely that many people argued against pursuing an ideas competition altogether. Undeterred by such opposition, FHL ultimately organised the competition internally with the help of Reed Kroloff, the editor of *Architecture* magazine.

The competition was open to anyone, and solicited entries from artists, architects, landscape architects, graphic designers, design students, urban designers and planners, and preservationists. The jury comprised a range of professionals, including Julie Bargmann, a landscape architect and professor; Vishaan Chakrabarti, a city planner at the New York Department of City Planning; Lee Compton, a community board member and neighbourhood resident; Lynne Cook, a curator at Dia Art Foundation; Steven Holl, an architect; Murray Moss, a design consultant; Marilyn Jordan Taylor, architect and partner at Skidmore, Owings & Merrill; Signe Nielsen, a landscape architect; Bernard Tschumi, an architect and dean of the Columbia University Graduate School of Architecture, Planning and Preservation; and Robert Hammond, co-founder of FHL. To help publicise the competition, a website was launched with the competition brief and submission instructions and

Figure 4.1 2003 ideas competition proposals
by Front Studio of New York (left), and
Nathalie Rinne of Vienna, Austria

parameters – an analogue process requiring entries to be submitted on 30-inch-by-40-inch boards, and mailed to New York for the juried review.

The response to FHL's open ideas competition – Designing the High Line – was overwhelming. More than 720 entries were received from 36 countries. At the time, it was one of the largest responses to an open ideas competition. Some of the most inspiring proposals included the idea for a mile-long lap pool, submitted by Nathalie Rinne, an architecture student from Vienna; a roller-coaster across the High Line, submitted by Yen Ha and Ostap Rudakevych of Front Studio (see Fig 4.1) and even a political manifesto entitled 'Park Prison Pool', which proposed building a prison within the steel beams of the High Line.

The Designing the High Line competition culminated in a large-scale exhibition in Grand Central Terminal's Vanderbilt Hall in the summer of 2003 (see Fig. 4.2). LOT-EK designed a lightweight structure to house the exhibition, which was visited by thousands of people during its two-week installation.

The ideas competition and exhibition put the High Line on the map, and quickly garnered international recognition and attention. New Yorkers began to pay more attention to the High Line, and started to follow its transformation, as well as FHL's progress. On the exhibition's opening night, Gifford Miller, then the speaker of the New York City Council, announced a $15.75m allocation to the High Line from the city. Within a year, by working with Mayor Michael Bloomberg's administration, a path to ownership for the city was established for the High Line structure, and work began on the second design competition.

Figure 4.2 Entries from the 2003 ideas competition were exhibited at Grand Central Terminal's Vanderbilt Hall in the summer of 2003

The High Line, master planning and design services – 2004 Request for Qualifications (RFQ) and Request for Proposals (RFP)

Following the first competition, the organisation recognised that it needed to bring in an in-house design professional. Peter Mullan, an architect at Polshek Partnership and a volunteer for FHL, was hired to help lead the design and planning initiatives of the organisation, including playing a key role in the design competition. Later on, Mullan played a vital role in managing the design and construction of the High Line and ensuring that the project was built on time and on budget.

In March 2004, the process of selecting a design team for the High Line master plan began. An RFQ was issued and attracted 51 responses. A shortlist of seven teams was announced in April; each received a two-stage RFP, and participated in interviews with the city and FHL. The first stage of the RFP required that each team develop a programmatic and design approach for the High Line.

In late May, four finalists were selected based on their responses to the first stage of the RFP. They were Zaha Hadid Architects (Hadid had just been awarded the Pritzker Prize) with Balmori Associates; James Corner Field Operations, Diller Scofidio + Renfro and Piet Oudolf; Steven Holl Architects with Hargreaves Associates; and TerraGRAM, a team made up of firms Michael Van Valkenburgh Associates, Julie Bargmann of D.I.R.T. studio and Beyer Blinder Belle. The second and final stage of the RFP required that each team articulate a full conceptual vision for the High Line, including strategies for landscape, paving, programming and access. Each team received a $25,000 stipend and was visited at their offices during the process.

The four teams submitted responses to the second stage of the RFP in early July, and presented their design proposals at the Center for Architecture in New York later that month. The competition submission required that each team develop a video animation as well as competition boards to be used in a public exhibition called 'Four Teams, Four Visions', that remained on display at the Center for Architecture through August (see Fig. 4.3).

The design competition was juried by a steering committee that was made up of representatives from the city and Friends of the High Line. The jury evaluated the proposals by the four finalists on the following key selection criteria: design excellence and vision, experience and track record, and team composition. Beyond these defined and fairly objective parameters, there was a question about which team would be the best fit for the project. The primary goal of the competition was to select a team, not a specific design. Whichever team was selected needed to be able to articulate a clear vision that could be rallied around.

Figure 4.3 Final four entries from the 2004 design competition included proposals by James Corner Field Operations, Diller Scofidio + Renfro, and Piet Oudolf (top), Zaha Hadid Architects with Balmori Associates (middle, left), TerraGRAM, a team made up of firms Michael Van Valkenburgh Associates, Julie Bargmann of D.I.R.T. studio, and Beyer Blinder Belle (middle, right), and Steven Holl Architects with Hargreaves Associates (bottom)

Figure 4.4 Competition board from James Corner Field Operations, Diller Scofidio + Renfro, and Piet Oudolf

In August 2004, the Steering Committee selected James Corner Field Operations, Diller Scofidio + Renfro and Piet Oudolf as the winning team. The team understood that there was something special about the High Line, and proposed a forward-looking vision that captured the spirit of the past as well as creating something new. Their competition proposal envisioned a simple walkway with plantings that evoked the wild landscape that took root on the High Line when it was abandoned. Their proposal posed a simple question: 'What will grow here?' This question considered everything from programmes and micro-climates to the ecosystems and economies that would play a role in (and impact the future of) the High Line. (See Fig. 4.4 and 4.5)

WHAT WILL GROW HERE ?

Inspired by the melancholic, unruly beauty of the High Line where nature has reclaimed a once vital piece of urban infrastructure, the team retools this industrial conveyance into a postindustrial instrument of leisure, life and growth. By changing the rules of engagement between plant life and pedestrians, our strategy of **AGRI-TECTURE** combines organic and building materials into gradients of changing proportions that accommodate the wild, the cultivated, the intimate, and the hyper-social. In stark contrast to the speed of Hudson River Park, this parallel linear experience is marked by slowness, distraction and an other-worldliness that preserves the strange character of the High Line. Providing flexibility and responsiveness to the changing needs, opportunities, and desires of the dynamic context, our proposal is designed to remain perpetually unfinished, sustaining emergent growth and change over time.

1 **AGRI-TECTURE:** A FLEXIBLE, RESPONSIVE SYSTEM OF MATERIAL ORGANIZATION WHERE DIVERSE ECOLOGIES MAY GROW.
The striated surface transitions from high intensity areas (100% hard) to richly vegetated biotopes (100% soft), with a variety of experiential gradients in-between.

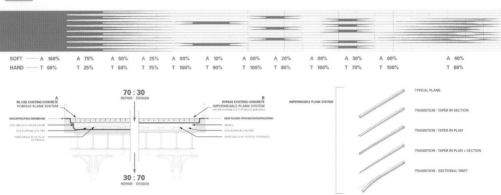

| SOFT | A 100% | A 75% | A 50% | A 25% | A 00% | A 10% | A 00% | A 20% | A 00% | A 30% | A 00% | A 40% |
| HARD | T 00% | T 25% | T 50% | T 75% | T 100% | T 90% | T 100% | T 80% | T 100% | T 70% | T 100% | T 60% |

2 A METHODOLOGY FOR CONSTRUCTING HARD SURFACES AND STRUCTURES AS MEANS OF PRODUCING DIVERSE SOCIAL AND NATURAL HABITATS. Designed as a continuous, single-surface, yet built from individual pre-cast units that may fold down to permit travel through the thick structural section of the High Line or fold up to pass over it without disturbing the natural "preserves."

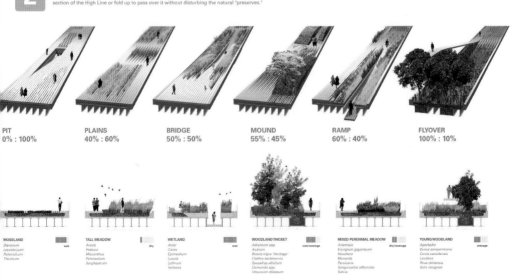

| PIT | PLAINS | BRIDGE | MOUND | RAMP | FLYOVER |
| 0% : 100% | 40% : 60% | 50% : 50% | 55% : 45% | 60% : 40% | 100% : 10% |

Figure 4.5 Competition rendering from James Corner Field Operations, Diller Scofidio + Renfro, and Piet Oudolf

In his review of the team's design, the *New York Times* architecture critic Nicolai Ouroussoff wrote:

'The preliminary design succeeds in preserving the High Line's tough industrial character without sentimentalising it. Instead, it creates a seamless blend of new and old, one rooted in the themes of decay and renewal that have long captivated the imagination of urban thinkers. [...] The strength of the Field Operations design is its ability to reflect a sense of communal mission without wiping away the site's historical character. These competing interests are balanced with exquisite delicacy. [...] The architects begin by creating a system of concrete planks that taper slightly at either end. The planks will be laid out along the High Line's deck in parallel bands, creating a pedestrian walkway that meanders back and forth as it traces the path of the elevated tracks, occasionally fading away to make room for a series of colorful gardens.'[1]

The 2004 design competition sought to build on the momentum of the 2003 ideas competition and public exhibition. While a number of hurdles remained, advancing the design continued to drive the organisation forward – and the further the design process advanced, the more the High Line was viewed as an inevitability rather than an uncertainty.

The role of community input and engagement

Following 9/11, there was a major shift in the public's engagement in and around discussions related to urban design and planning. For the first time in many years, there was a willingness to have a discourse about urbanism in New York, which was primarily driven by the large-scale master-planning competition for the site of the World Trade Center. The High Line took a lot of energy from that, and it propelled the project forward from the early days of FHL's founding in 1999.

FHL understood early on that public engagement would be an important way to win – and ultimately sustain – support for the High Line, both before and after the park opened. The design competition showed that the public could get behind the idea of transforming the old tracks into a viable public space, which helped move the project forward. But FHL knew it had to continue to build on that support for the park to realise its full potential – work that its staff continue to undertake.

Following the design competition, FHL organised more than a dozen community input sessions to solicit opinions about the concepts from neighbourhood residents. West Chelsea is home to two large low-income housing developments – Fulton Houses and Chelsea-Elliott Houses – and FHL knew it was important to engage with all community leaders and members throughout the design process to ensure there would be a sense of ownership when the park ultimately opened.

After the park opened in 2009, FHL assessed that original goal and realised that not everyone in the community felt welcome on the High Line. The organisation pivoted its community engagement strategy, building out its cultural programming offerings, establishing an employment programme for local teens, and partnering with local public schools and other community organisations to bring more West Chelsea residents to the park.

This increased focus on neighbourhood residents has helped diversify the park's visitors: in 2015, more than 2 million New Yorkers visited the High Line – 44% of whom were people of colour. And FHL is still engaging community residents in the future direction of the park by working with its Neighbors Council on the design and usage plans of the ground-level 18th Street Plaza, on which construction will begin in 2018.

Over the years, other community leaders, designers and city officials have turned to FHL for advice or input on similar projects they want to develop in their own cities. In 2016, FHL established the High Line Network, a group of nearly 20 infrastructure reuse projects across North America whose members gather several times a year to share best practices and challenges, as well as envision what these projects, as a network, can achieve together. As the role of public spaces in cities becomes more important – and more accountable to city residents – FHL hopes the network will help its members (as well as the movement as a whole) learn to work in the most productive way with a range of stakeholders to help shape their shared communities.

Note

1 Nicolai Ouroussoff: "An Appraisal; Gardens in the Air Where the Rail Once Ran" http://www.nytimes.com/2004/08/12/arts/an-appraisal-gardens-in-the-air-where-the-rail-once-ran.html

STRATEGIEN FÜR KREUZBERG: RELOCATING THE URBAN REGENERATION DEBATES INTO THE NEIGHBOURHOOD

Florian Kossak

A competition's background

Any Berlin visitor taking the short stroll through the lively Wrangelstrasse in the heart of Kreuzberg will associate it with the quintessential Berlin street. Lined with five-storey-high tenement buildings, the formerly infamous *Mietskasernen* (rental barracks) from the last two decades of the 19th century features a particular *Kreuzberger Mischung*, a functional mixture of residential with shops and small workshops at ground level facing the street, and smaller production places in the courtyards and part of the upper floors of the back buildings.

Almost halfway along Wrangelstrasse one passes Oppelner Strasse, a crossing with widened pedestrian zones in front of the corner houses, pavements and streets, with carefully laid-out patterns made of small cobblestones forming a *Spielstrasse* (play street) and planters that rise smoothly out of the ground providing seating opportunities, and preventing cars from parking. Plastic chairs and timber benches are placed in front of cafes and restaurants, Turkish and German flags hang between trees, a small group of men stands in front of an internet shop, children cycle on the road.

What appears to be an ordinary street scene in one of the now trendy, traditionally working-class areas of Berlin – an expression of textbook urbanity

– would not have been in existence today had it not been for a ground-breaking competition through which new forms of urban regeneration had been developed and tested. This competition is the *Strategien für Kreuzberg* (Strategies for Kreuzberg), dating from 1977/78.

Towards the mid-1970s, the eastern part of Berlin-Kreuzberg, called SO36,[1] with its traditional working-class housing areas around the former railway goods station Görlitzer Bahnhof, became – although largely saved from any war damage – a so-called 'problem zone'[2] of West Berlin. Economically, socially and politically it was an 'urban blindspot' in the post-war redevelopments of West Berlin. Geographically, it was isolated from the rest of the city after the construction of the Berlin Wall. Economically, it had lost its former focal point, the now disused Görtlitzer Bahnhof, and was increasingly losing small businesses in functionally mixed tenement buildings. The building stock, over 90% of which was built before 1919, was mostly dilapidated through decades of underinvestment; 40% of the units were without toilets or baths inside the flats. Culturally, the area was very diverse, with a large, mostly Turkish, migrant population, a growing population of young people looking for an alternative lifestyle, and the established, ageing and diminishing working-class population.

The isolated position of West Berlin within the territory of the GDR left the city economy heavily dependent on West German subsidies. Through the so-called Berlinhilfegesetz (Berlin Support Act) from 1964, the state actively provided tax incentives for investment, employment and consumption in order to keep West Berlin on a lifeline and remain the *Schaufenster des Westens* (shop window of the West) in the ideological battle of the two economic and political systems which opposed each other in the city.[3] In terms of urban regeneration, the city was subjected to the so-called Stadterneuerungsprogramm or City Renewal Programme ratified by the SPD-led[4] Berlin Senate in 1963. It legally framed the large-scale comprehensive redevelopment – read total demolition of tens of thousands of units in run-down, de-invested, inner city housing areas – and the relocation of its population to newly built housing estates in the outer suburbs of West Berlin. In parallel, and on a smaller scale, modernist housing schemes were constructed on 'cleared' inner city areas, mostly neglecting the historical urban block structure.[5]

Figure 4.6
Cover of the *Strategien für Kreuzberg*
competition brief brochure. The
cover image shows the dilapidated
condition of a typical 1870s tenement
building in Berlin-Kreuzberg

An important shift in planning principles

However, this housing and urban regeneration approach encountered
increasing opposition from the late 1960s onwards,[6] which ultimately led to a
dramatic change in West Berlin's planning culture. This involved moving away
from a bulldozer mentality to a position that respected the existing building
fabric and its residents' desire to play a role in urban transformation processes.
It was in this situation that the Berlin Senate, after intense lobbying of parish
priest Klaus Duntze and local politician Gerd Wartenberg, initiated the two-
stage open ideas competition *Strategien für Kreuzberg* in March 1977.[7]

According to Duntze, there were:

> *'several key reasons not to continue the practice of a comprehensive
> redevelopment ... One reason is certainly the disastrous experience with
> the effects of the regeneration practice to that date: displacement of
> the old population from the redevelopment areas, the enormous costs
> for purchasing and preparing the plots [for redevelopment] as well as
> the high rental costs for the relocated residents. [...] Another reason
> is the [now] missing financial contingency for such large-scale urban
> redevelopment programmes as they have been conducted in West
> Berlin up to that point [...]. The most important reason would be that the*

protestant church made [...] the proposal for an urban renewal project in which the affected community would be involved through co-planning, co-realisation, and co-ownership.'[8]

Duntze's third reason, and the mentioning of the three principles of 'co-planning, co-realisation, and co-ownership', already allude to the very different character and processes that the *Strategien* was supposed to apply in contrast to previous urban regeneration practice. And while there were still several 'ordinary' professional competitions happening exactly at the same time just several blocks further west, in the so-called SKKT regeneration area around Kottbusser Tor,[9] the Berlin Senate was aiming here for the *Strategien* to 'prepare, with the participation of all citizens, the preconditions for an urban development – and improvement process whose guiding principles would build upon the continuity of the current conditions in the neighbourhoods'.[10] The competition brief was asking contributors to 'develop new approaches and aims for the reinvigoration of the neighbourhoods north and south of the former Görlitzer Bahnhof in Berlin-Kreuzberg as well as pick up on existing perspectives in order to develop exemplary strategies for the affected population'.[11] Asking for strategies instead of building projects, addressing the affected population instead of owner or institutional stakeholders,

Figure 4.7 Double-page map from the competition brief brochure showing the 'SfK' area (yellow) in the wider spatial context of Berlin. The area is located at the very eastern part of the Kreuzberg district (yellow line). The spatial isolation of the SfK area is not only heightened by the Berlin Wall, which severed its formerly close relation to the historic city centre, but also by the large railway areas (hatched) which limit the access to the Kreuzberg district from the new West-Berlin centre

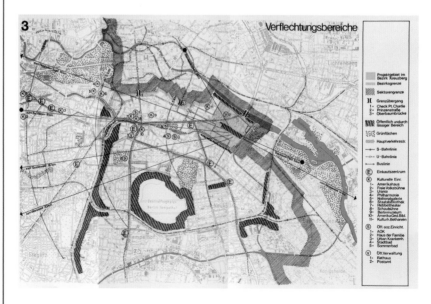

foregrounding continuity – read also social continuity without the removal
of existing tenants and destruction of grown communities – presents a
significant shift in Berlin's urban renewal approach of the time.

And yet the truly innovative moment of this competition resides less in its
overall ambition for a different outcome than in its radical and open process
framework. Whereas community consultation had become a more or less
superficial alibi function of urban regeneration processes and their associated
professional competitions, from the early 1970s onwards, the *Strategien* took
an altogether different approach. Rather than inviting a selected number of
urban practitioners, ie architects and planners, the *Strategien* allowed, as the
almost 100-page-long competition briefing document states, participation
by 'all individuals, initiatives and institutions in the affected area – as long as
they are willing and able to approach the tasks of the projects in their entirety
– as well as all individuals or groups (ie community groups, citizens forums,
action groups etc) with theoretical or practical experience in the area of urban
development or urban improvement'.[12]

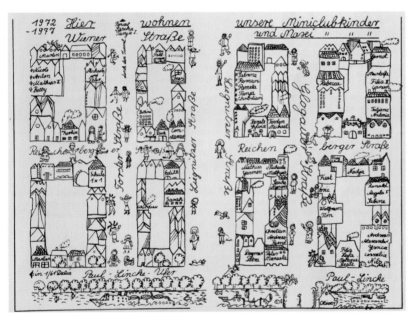

Figure 4.8 'This is where our Miniclub and Maxiclub kids live.' This drawing, also published in the competition brief
brochure, illustrates the emphasis that '*Strategien*' put on the inclusion of all residents and their needs in the strategic
rethinking of this neighbourhood

Although there is still a majority of wide-ranging, professional participants, in particular among the finally selected 11 projects, this opening up of the competition can be regarded as partially successful. The documentation of the *Strategien* process and project results[13] states that 45% of the total 281 authors of the 129 submitted entries weren't architects or planners (36%), sociologists or pedagogues (14%), or other social scientists (5%). A clear majority of participants, 71%, came from West Berlin, of which 12% came directly from the actual project area SO36, and a further 10% from the Kreuzberg borough.[14] A number of very diverse, pre-existing groups and institutions in the project area, such as Kinderspielkreis Südost ev (play circle), Heinrich-Hanselmann-Schule (local primary school), Arbeitsgemeinschaft SO36 der CDU Kreuzberg (local branch of the Christian Democratic Party) and Gemeindekirchenrat der Tabor-Kirchengemeinde (parish council of the Tabor Church), contributed with project entries to the *Strategien*.

But this deliberate inclusion of lay people in the competition process happened not only on the side of the participants. Of even greater significance is the actual jury process, in particular, the composition of the judging panel itself. Rather than having a then normal-jury composition,[15] the *Strategien* installed a so-called Project Commission consisting of 19 local lay members (and the same number of non-voting deputies), two representatives of private landlords and public housing associations, and 13 members of the borough, city and planning office authorities. The members of the lay group represented defined groups[16] in their majority traditionally working- and lower-middle-class citizens that had dominated the population of this part of Kreuzberg for the past 100 years, and were thus a social mirror of the *Kreuzberger Mischung*. A younger generation of new, 'alternative' residents of Kreuzberg, who came to the area towards the end of the 1970s, and who would play a vital role in the squatting movement of the early 1980s, have (at least on this organisational level) only a minor role. There are also only six representatives with a migration background in the commission, despite migrants forming (even in the 1970s) approximately 25% of the population in the *Strategien* area – an under-representation which is even more noticeable in the submitted projects of the *Strategien* competition. However, what is crucial in terms of this composition is that the group of local residents, the so-called lay people, had the voting majority over the group of experts and political representatives.

An alternative urban model

The Project Commission started their work with initial preparatory meetings in March and April 1977, moving towards an intensive jury phase during the first half of August. During this five-month period, the Project Commission and sub-groups had over 100 meetings in total,[17] discussing each entry at length. After four rounds of elimination, 11 projects were selected for further development in a second phase. The length of this process was exceptional, in particular when comparing it to the two days it took the jury to decide the winning project in the competition in the SKKT competition around Oranienplatz in the same year.[18] The selection process was not, however, without its controversies, as particularly in the final decision-making sessions, the lay groups were confronted with the well-oiled 'bureaucratic machinery'[19] of the professional and political commission members.

And yet, the variety of the 11 selected projects is testimony to a radical shift in thinking about new strategies and projects for urban regeneration, informed and driven by the interest of the affected residents of the *Strategien* area. The projects included propositions for community and social infrastructure, such as the community association Verein SO36, the Youth Centre Kreuzberg, the Information Centre Living and Dwelling Otur ve Yasa for Turkish residents, and a Vocational Apprenticeship Institute.[20] There were also proposals for new ownership models and participatory concepts of housing stock regeneration, as well as concrete building proposals for a new 'Citizens Park on the former Görlitzer Bahnhof' or the 'Public Real Improvement Oppelner Strasse', already mentioned in the introduction of this essay.

The 11 selected projects were first publicly exhibited and presented to the wider public through evening talks in a converted circus tent on Spreewaldplatz. At the end of September 1977, the winning project teams moved into empty shops throughout the project area, in order to work further on their proposals in direct exchange with local residents and affected communities.[21] This second phase lasted almost five months; it involved regular meetings of the Project Commission sub-groups before the projects were submitted for a second jury round in February 1978. The revised projects were then publicly exhibited and debated throughout the project area. It was not until late December 1978 that the results of this second, realisation phase were finally ratified by the Berlin Senate.

Figure 4.9 Axonometric drawing of the winning entry by Heinz-Jörg and Monika Reiher that proposed a public realm improvement for the Oppelner Strasse crossing as a galvanizing moment in the regeneration of the Strategien area

The significance of this competition, and its public form of negotiations through forums, workshops and exhibitions, had already been recognised in some early reports about the *Strategien*. Ueli Schäfer wrote in the Swiss magazine *Bauen+Wohnen* that 'in a few years' time we will be able to assert that a truly important competition took place in Berlin-Kreuzberg: The attempt to "regenerate" a run-down inner city area not through top-down, preconceived architecture and planning doctrine, but by including everybody involved (residents, administration, competition contributors) in a thought- and decision-making process'.[22] And Neal Pierce of the *Washington Post* predicted that, '... if [the Strategies for Kreuzberg] succeeds in major part, an international model may well have been set: of how even the most depressed neighbourhood can be revived, of ways to draw in and motivate alienated citizens, of using a competition to meld the ideas of bright young professionals with the realities of life at the neighbourhood level'.[23]

Today, local politicians, planners and architects operate almost automatically with concepts of participation in urban regeneration processes; one could consider the *Strategien für Kreuzberg*'s most lasting effect on architecture and planning in Berlin (and beyond) to be that it initiated the successful demonstration of these new approaches, which contributed to making Kreuzberg the alternative urban model that still exists today.

The *Strategien* should be regarded as a guiding example for a growing praxis of experimental exhibitions, competitions and public negotiations of urban development. These moments of praxis can become the prime medium and locale for processes of translation between different cultures or disciplinarily defined languages, for example, between architectural and planning disciplines and engaged public or political bodies.[24] They not only occupy the role of 'mediator' or 'translator' of the complexities of the production processes of architecture and urban planning into a public setting; they transgress beyond being localities within which such mediation can take place to become the spatial and social settings that make conversations and negotiations between users and policy makers, top and bottom, finance and ambitions, the 'real' and the 'desired', possible.

Notes

1 So36 stands for the then postal code, *Süd-Ost* [south-east] 36.

2 *Strategien für Kreuzberg*, ed. Hanno Klein (Berlin: Senator für Bau- und Wohnungswesen, 1977), 3.

3 See Emily Pugh, *Architecture, Politics & Identity in Divided Berlin* (Pittsburgh: University of Pittsburgh Press, 2014).

4 Social Democratic Party.

5 See Harald Bodenschatz, Volker Heise and Jochen Korfmacher, *Schluß mit der Zerstörung? Stadterneuerung und Städtische Opposition in West-Berlin, Amsterdam und London* (Gießen: Anabas Verlag, 1983).

6 First formulated in the 1969 exhibition *'Diagnose zum Bauen in West-Berlin'* at the Technical University Berlin. See Florian Kossak 'Aktion 507 – Politics become Theory become Praxis', in *This Thing Called Theory*, eds Teresa Stoppani et al. (New york: Routledge, 2016), 137–146.

7 3 March 1977 publication of the competition brief.

8 Arch+ 34, 14.

9 Harald Bodenschatz et al., *Schluß mit der Zerstörung?* 100–105.

10 *Strategien für Kreuzberg*, ed. Hanno Klein, 3.

11 *Strategien für Kreuzberg*, ed. Hanno Klein, 3.

12 *Strategien für Kreuzberg*, ed. Hanno Klein, 4.

13 Strategien für Kreuzberg 1. *Verfahren und Projektergebnisse*, ed. Hanno Klein (Berlin: Senator Für Bau- und Wohnungswesen, 1978).

14 19% Came from West Germany, 10% from abroad (in particular from Switzerland, Austria and the UK). There aren't any conclusive figures as to whether the 22% from the Kreuzberg area were predominantly also part of the 45% non-professionals.

15 A jury would have normally consisted of approximately six professional (ie architects, planners) members and approximately five political or stakeholder (i.E. Councillors, housing associations) members, plus a range of non-voting consulting experts.

16 The lay groups represented in the Project Commission were classed as 'Tenants', 'Employees', 'Senior Citizens', 'Trade', 'Immigrants', 'Youth', 'Education', 'Action Groups', 'Church', 'Gardeners' and 'Charities', and included a pest-controller, a job-seeker, several carpenters, a medical technician, an engineer, several pensioners, a saddle-maker, a publican, several shop-owners and merchants, a baker, a bank clerk, a typesetter, two teachers and one artist.

17 The figure is given by project commission member Günter Nausedat in his column *'Durch die Molle betrachtet', Südost Express*, issue 3, 1978, 20.

18 Anon. 'Sanierungsgebiet Oranienstraße – Stadtzerstörung wie bisher nur mit anderen Fassaden?' *Südost Express*, issue 4, 1978, 10.

19 Nausedat, *'Durch die Molle betrachtet'*, 20.

20 The Vocational Apprenticeship Institute (or *Ausbildungswerk* e.V.) gives unemployed youth in Kreuzberg the opportunity to get a professional qualification as a carpenter, electrician, plumber or builder. Considering that the ongoing regeneration of Kreuzberg and its dilapidated housing stock required an increased number of qualified workers, it also aimed at allowing those living in the area to play a substantial part within this process, enabling them to provide services and products that are useful for themselves and their immediate environment. The *Ausbildungswerk* still operates today.

21 A description of the work in six of those shops can be found in anon. 'Läden der "Strategien für Kreuzberg" stellen sich vor', *Südost Express*, December 1977, 3.

22 Schäfer, 'Strategien für Kreuzberg, Berlin', Bauen+Wohnen, vol 32, no 1, 1978, 43.

23 Neal Pierce, 'A Neighborhood Contest Beside the Berlin Wall', Washington Post, February 1978, in *Strategien für Kreuzberg 1. Verfahren und Projektergebnisse*, ed. Hanno Klein (Berlin: Senator für bau- und Wohnungswesen, 1978), 68.

24 Florian kossak, 'The Real Beside the Real: The Laboratory Exhibition and The Experimental Production of Architecture', thesis, Edinburgh College of Art, 2008; see also *Exhibitions and the Development of Modern Planning Culture*, eds Robert Freestone and Marco Amati (Farnham: Ashgate, 2014).

CHAPTER 17

COMMUNITY BEFORE COMPETITIONS

Discussion with Peter Wynne Rees

Question (Q): How would you describe politics in the context of your past role as the chief planner for the City of London?

Peter Wynne Rees (PWR): Of my 45 years of professional career, 29 were spent directing the planning of the City of London, or to be more accurate, the regeneration of the City of London. Working for the City Corporation, I was working for the only local authority in the country that did not have party politics. All elected members served as independent members. Therefore, policy creation was a matter for professional officers. Members took the role of the company board, reviewing the proposals put forward by the officers. Through a process of interrogation and debate, they decided on the way to go forward. That's different from other local authorities, where policy is led by party political manifesto and delivered through a structure where officers realise the aspirations of the elected members. I am coming at this from an unusual point of view: that of a professional planner in the public service who had the opportunity to lead change.

Q: What is the process by which architecture is procured in the City of London, and what was your role?

PWR: Architectural procurement is in the remit of the developer, not the planning system. It is a matter for the owner of the site, advised by their planning consultants and property advisers. However, I cannot say that I didn't influence the process, because I encouraged developers in the City to go and see (and choose from) a broad range of architects, and to study recent projects that they found successful. When asked for advice on shortlisting, I encouraged diversity, with a couple of 'business practices' to provide a quote-efficient approach and some leading architects with international awards and headlines. Developers should also look at the results of the RIBA and other awards for up-and-coming practices of interest to provide fresh thinking and ingenious design ideas. I was occasionally asked to help choose between alternative design proposals, and I agreed only on condition that the material was presented without identifying the architects. Although I must admit the presentation styles of some practices are rather distinctive, I sought to advise developers purely from the point of view of the planner representing the local neighbourhood, and above all, the community. From my point of view, the best design project is one where the planner, the architect and the developer sit down together at the outset. The developer has a brief, quite obviously, but the planner also has a brief for the neighbourhood and community. Until the architect is in possession of both briefs, he or she is not in a position to start designing. It is a synthesis of the planner's and the developer's briefs that provides the raw material from which a good design is produced. An architect that works *in vitro*, purely for his or her client and not for the benefit of the community or the locale, is not going to produce the best buildings. This is one of my fundamental concerns about the inadequacies of architecture competitions: they encourage working *in vitro* without a fully briefed start to a design project.

Q: In open competitions, at least, architects have the chance to submit their ideas and win?

PWR: That's not true; architects don't have a balanced chance. If you design the most contextual, the most sensitive, most invisible building, you are unlikely to win an architecture competition. It is the flamboyant or distinctive designs that have the best chance. So a competition encourages a particular kind of architecture. It doesn't encourage place and community focused architecture, it encourages architecture that will attract the attention of the jury – in other words, architecture for other architects.

Q: You have already stated your distrust of competitions, and I wonder whether you also discard experimentation, a concept that relates to scientific thinking and has been associated with competitions.

PWR: I agree that architecture competitions have been a source of new ideas and experimentation. Now, if you think of other branches of human endeavour, I was going to say sciences, most experimentation is carried out on prototypes. It is carried out in laboratories, not in the real world and on real people; at least not until the technique is proved or at a very advanced stage. One of our problems in architecture is that every building is its own prototype. This affects people's appreciation of architecture as they see fundamental issues arising on many projects. Such was the case in the development of the 'Walkie-Scorchie', one of the City towers. But as I explain, when leading tours around the City, if this had been a new aircraft they would have built 20 prototypes before it first flew, and it wouldn't have gone into production until it was thoroughly tested and modified. You cannot do that with a building, so it is not surprising things occasionally go wrong. There are weaknesses in a system which encourages experiment and innovation, straight off, without the chance to test and prototype, as it were, in the laboratory.

The media have encouraged a large part of society to seek success through 'discovery' and instant fame rather than hard work and experience. The architecture competition is a precursor of this kind of thinking: 'if we submit our ideas to enough architecture competitions we will eventually be discovered and become successful'. From obscurity to fame through the One Big Win.

I have seen many brilliant architectural practices put a huge amount of their life into architecture competitions, wasting so much of their talent on a system which is a lottery. The competition winner is not necessarily the best design. It may be the most appealing, obvious or flamboyant design, but it is not necessarily the best solution. The more talent that

is squandered on trying to win competitions, the less we have available for everyday buildings and small projects which improve architecture across the piece.

I am a strong supporter of awards for small projects, which can be the stepping stone to major work. However small, the awarded project demonstrates what you can do. As one of the chairs of the RIBA Awards in 2015, I reviewed the projects in the East Midlands region. My metro-centric experience led me to anticipate a lower level of design ingenuity and architectural quality, but I was amazed by the passion shown by young architects working on small projects. A sensitively deferential studio outbuilding was tucked among the houses in a small village. A local architect and developer had produced a small apartment block in the middle of a historic Derbyshire town which involved reopening the local quarry and employing local metalworkers to craft the metalwork for the building while producing a contemporary design. Working in those circumstances, with client and local suppliers unused to the benefits of architectural quality, was just as award-worthy as producing an attention-seeking competition submission. This was a quality of work I had not anticipated. The award system provided the mechanism for discovering architectural talent through practice. A competition can demonstrate innovative design thinking. But even a small implemented project demonstrates ability not only in thinking [up] the design, but in motivating a team to realise it.

Q: It seems that young architects are leaving behind the idea of winning competitions by submitting impressive projects. As you mentioned, young practices choose to, or by necessity, work in small projects at the local level. Do you think education reflects this change?

PWR: As Professor of Places and City Planning at the Bartlett [UCL], I am interested to see the difference between the way we educate planners and architects in Britain. There seems to be a widely held belief that architecture students are best educated in a protective bubble, away from the constraints of the real world, in order to intensify the flavour of their creative juices. I believe that design skill and creative intensity are increased by introducing more constraints and contextual realism into projects. I find that planning students respond to the challenge admirably when they are confronted with real places and real issues; and I think architecture students are no different. Architecture education and architecture competitions are strongly linked; those involved in architecture education often see the competition process as their route to recognition, and encourage

their students in this belief. We cannot view the shortcomings of architecture competitions in isolation from the way we educate our architects and prime their expectations of overnight success.

Q: Despite consultation processes, communities or the general public seem unable to make their voices heard as to how the built environment is currently shaped by developers. Could ideas architecture competitions help the public visualise and safely experiment with alternatives?

PWR: It might be more useful to the general community to have competitions for planning strategies rather than for architectural projects. These could explore the implications of alternative mixtures and dispositions of land use and building forms. They would inform and involve people in the possibilities and choices inherent in place-making. The public should be involved in the process of change at the earliest stage, and before the architect becomes involved. It would be interesting to turn things around and allow the public to submit entries to these competitions with the architects as judges. Maybe we should replace architecture competitions with community competitions.

194

CHAPTER 18

COMPETITIONS AND EDUCATIONAL STRUCTURES

Discussion with Craig Stott and Simon Warren

Question (Q): Project Office (PO), the consultancy situated between academia and practice you have been directing since 2013, launched an alumni ideas competition for the Leeds Beckett University Sustainable Technologies and Landscape Research Centre (STaLRC) in 2016. Have you used the architecture competition format before, and how does it fit with the PO principles?

Figure 4.10 Completed NWCC Building

Craig Stott (CS) and Simon Warren (SW), Project Office directors: 'Project Office is a design and research collaboration of staff and students based within the Leeds School of Architecture, Leeds Beckett University. It is an architecture consultancy concerned with ethical, social and resilient architecture and design. We work with like-minded communities, organisations and individuals.'[1] It has successfully led a number of student–community involvement projects, including the delivery of the Big Lottery-funded New Wortley Community Centre (NWCC), which started as a competition.

Project Office operates as a conduit to provide students with a construction-led education through the vehicle of 'live projects', as defined by Rachel Sara.[2] PO has been combining the architectural competition and live project to situate bespoke learning environments since 2009, with both undergraduate and postgraduate students. Such interventions are usually done over a short period of time within a design studio module, and students achieve credits for their endeavours. Students often work in teams, and a judging panel of tutors and clients rank the work. To date, PO has overseen the construction of two winning competition designs, providing a range of students [with] invaluable experience relating to design, construction detailing and hands-on construction, as well as the bolstering of CVs.

Figure 4.11 Morley Newlands Playscape

Q: Why did you choose the format of a competition to experiment with alumni pedagogy?

CS & SW: Following the successful use of competitions for undergraduate and postgraduate architecture students, PO entertained the idea of experimenting by using the competition format to tackle a different problem; namely, that the institution's association with its students is almost severed once they become alumni. By extending pedagogy through a competition, new possibilities have arisen between this school of architecture and its recent former students who sit at a paradox's apex: they are the most affected by the tensions and contradictions of practice versus academy, having landed in practice with the realities of financial and client pressures after previously spending five years in full-time architectural education. The juxtaposition is severe, meaning recent graduates are a fertile educational opportunity. The architectural competition, used as a pedagogic tool, is harnessed in a post-formal educational setting. An intended output, for example, is that alumni competitions can be legitimately situated in the Continuing Professional Development (CPD) framework, viably enabling UK schools of architecture to participate, fulfilling a professional developmental remit.

Q: Why did you decide to organise the STaLRC as a competition, and how was the competition process transformed into an educational tool?

CS & SW: Leeds Beckett University appointed PO to act as architect and contract administrator for all RIBA Work Stages of the STaLRC, beginning at Stage 1 with definition of the brief and a total budget of £819,000. Through discussion it was determined that, because of the tight timescales involved, the scale and complexity of the project being appropriate, and the opportunity for PO to appoint the winning team as consultants, the concept design stage for STaLRC should be realised through a competition for Leeds School of Architecture landscape architecture and architecture alumni. A prize fund of £500 was made available to be distributed at the judges' discretion, and the winning entrant would be invited to work as a paid consultant to PO on the remainder of the project. In proposing a competition, we were aware of the paradoxical situation that this had created.[3] Consequently, the STaLRC architectural competition became a relevant tool to push the boundaries of live project education as it confronts the contradictions of advancing architectural knowledge, experimentation and production of real work for a client. Each stage of the competition was treated as an educational tool.

To initiate the alumni competition, a briefing pack needed producing for distribution. Continuing PO's pedagogical approach of live project learning, this necessity became an opportunity. In January 2016, five BA2 students, who chose to undergo their placement[4] with PO, were tasked with creating the briefing pack for the competition. Through undertaking the required initial research and site enquiries, and collating existing data and reports, the students constructed a Design Guide, which acted as competition brief to be sent out to all alumni alongside the Rules of Engagement and a detailed CAD map of the site. This was distributed via email in early April 2016 to all alumni from Parts 1, 2 and 3 from the previous five years.

Alumni competitors, able to work as individuals or in teams, had three weeks to produce four A3 concept design sheets. Content was at the entrants' discretion, but guidance suggested including relevant information allowing the judges a

Figure 4.12 Guide review session.

Figure 4.13 Page from the Design Guide

clear understanding of the project; in addition, clearly expressed ideas for minimising both cost and energy consumption during construction and in-use would be favourably considered. An open site visit was organised for the end of week one, which was well attended and offered the competitors a key insight into the unique location of the project, and the beauty in which their proposition would nestle. This proved significant, as four of the five shortlisted schemes were submitted by those who visited the site and entered solutions which truly sought to embed themselves as elements within the landscape. The timescale was purposely tight. Given that the majority of entrants would be employed full time, PO estimated three weeks of free time was analogous to a high-pressured office situation producing a feasibility study. Four A3 sheets meant the output was not significant, and again in keeping

with office procedure. One aspect left open by PO, but which proved to be significant, was the composition of teams. None of the shortlisted entries were submitted by individuals. In practice, it is rare for young architects in the early stages of their career to be working in isolation. This reflects another virtue of the live project environment – collaboration is at the heart of the production as opposed to the singular authorship of a traditional design studio. Entrants self-selected groups within their alumni to work together.

Thirteen entries were received from a strong array of alumni. To celebrate and judge the work, PO organised a publicly open and advertised awards night where all schemes entered into the competition were displayed, and their contributors invited. Prior to the event, the steering group (under the guidance of PO) selected five shortlisted schemes to present their

Figure 4.14 Alumni competition site visit

Figure 4.15 Competition judging event
Figure 4.16 Competition winners

project at the awards evening. Each team had their A3 sheets projected and ten minutes to talk through their proposal, followed by a ten-minute session where the judges asked difficult questions to ensure they fully understood the scheme. The event was a tremendous success, with the university's head of estates, pro vice-chancellor and dean of the Faculty of Arts, Environment & Technology being included as members of the judging panel. A team of three alumni were unanimously chosen winners. All members are currently employed in architecture practices across the north of England and undertook their Parts 1 and 2 (and are currently studying Part 3) at the Leeds School of Architecture. The three alumni are now working as paid consultants to PO, upon the planning design phase, with a submission intended for February 2017.

PO began to consider how the working relationship was now different between former students and us as former tutors through the process of working together in this new situation. The winning team felt that working with PO was the next progression in a long-standing relationship; we were working alongside each other professionally, contributing towards a singular output. The defining difference compared to a traditional practice condition is that PO did not lose its role as educators; what has happened is that we have realised that we are all learners together, but there remains, in PO's role, the responsibility to be educators. The relationship the alumni describe is almost identical to that which Susan Imel espouses when explaining the concept of Collaborative Learning in adult education.[5] The key concepts relate to the hierarchy between facilitators and learners being eliminated, and in so doing both become active participants in the educational process. In such an arrangement, Imel suggests that while both the 'facilitators and learners are jointly responsible for establishing the environment for activity, it is the responsibility of the facilitator to take the lead'. This is exactly the situation PO and the winning alumni team are currently in, working together as a team continually attempting to address the paradox of continued alumni education with the realisation of live project delivery.

Architecture competitions have also long been criticised for the way they take advantage of well-meaning architects, and their wastefulness of unsuccessful entries. In the educational setting, this is avoided as the whole process is about learning, and the PO and client respected the process by paying an honorarium to all entrants.

The final element of PO's approach to alumni competitions is the giving of detailed and individual feedback. Normal competition entrants do not expect to receive any feedback from the competition organisers about the merits of their work. However, it is not unusual for winners, runners up and commended entries to receive some commentary on their endeavours through brief feedback. In this situation, feedback has two purposes: first, to disseminate the competition to a wider audience through press releases or magazine articles, second, for the non-winning but placed entrants, to soften the blow of not winning.

A completely different use of feedback is required in the alumni competition where the entrants' learning experience is of equal importance to the work produced. Consequently, feedback for the STaLRC project was written in detail by PO for each of the 13 entries. As a learning exercise for alumni it was essential that feedback on their entries was diligently undertaken, and useful for them in critiquing their work and developing as young professionals.

The feedback was split into three categories: Positive Aspects, Areas to Develop and Additional Comments.

We wanted each competitor to benefit from the judges' view, but also have an appraisal of their work as if PO were acting in a modified tutor/student relationship. The feedback was in the formative assessment tradition,[6] consistent in schools of architecture, that alumni would have been familiar with in their five years of formal architectural education. Continuing this into alumni education appears at odds with students' fledging, but we think that formative feedback could be continued in a more structured way in working life, perhaps linked into an annual review system by the employers. Through charting the competition stages and reflections of participants, this project is the first step in developing PO's methodology for alumni engagement through pedagogically driven design competitions.

Q: What do you consider to be the future engagement of Project Office with competitions?

CS & SW: PO exists because we believe the complexities facing architects are often oversimplified in architectural education, so that the skills, problem-solving methods, people relationships and real-life complexities necessary to successfully navigate a life in practice are not sufficiently learned, and are therefore neither framed nor reflected upon intellectually. The work PO undertakes, and the

Figure 4.17 Winning entry

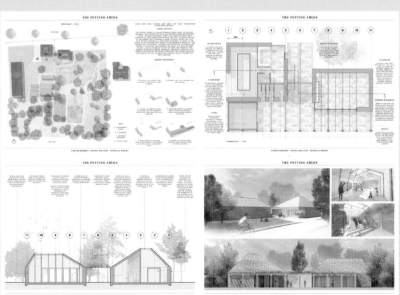

related situated learning in the design studio, are intended to address these shortfalls, with competitions forming part of the strategy, as the format is a practical way to deliver the initial design work of a live project; however, this approach is also motivated by pedagogy in that the learning environment simulates aspects of architectural practice. The STaLRC alumni competition success supports the suggestion that alumni competitions are a good platform for continued engagement with students; in maintaining contact with its alumni, PO has managed to extend architectural pedagogy by placing a value on the transition between education and profession. Fledgling professionals, unencumbered by the specificity of ARB (Architects Registration Board) criteria or the pressures of practice, are free to expand and test their abilities within a framework of trust. The learning outcomes of participants are of equal importance to the production (and quality) of the entries, thus with comprehensive feedback provided, every entrant is able to use the process to further their abilities and understanding. There exists a unique moment of critical thinking where new knowledge can be generated as academic organisers engage with the creative power of alumni graduates.

Notes

1   Craig Stott and Simon Warren, in *Project Office*, Vol 1 (Leeds: 2014).

2   Rachel Sara defines Live Projects as 'a type of design project that is distinct from a typical studio project in its engagement of real clients or users, in real-time settings. Students are taken out of the studio setting, and repositioned in the 'real world'. This external involvement tends to result in students producing something that is of value to the client/user group, which might range from ideas, feasibility reports, or research, to a completed design scheme, a construction or other intervention.' Rachel Sara, *Live Project Good Practice: A Guide for the Implementation of Live Projects* (York: Higher Education Academy, 2006).

3   'Competitions are driven by the desire to go beyond what already exists – unthought-of architecture – whereas commissions are mostly demand-driven and often by those of the market', Farshid Moussavi. 'Viewpoints: Farshid Moussavi on Competitions', *The Architectural Review* [online] available at: http://www.architectural-review.com/view/ viewpoints/viewpoint-farshid-moussavi/8641757. article?blocktitle=Viewpoints&contentID=6120.

4   Each year, the architecture course organises a week-long work placement scheme for undergraduates to experience practice at local architecture firms.

5   Susan Imel, 'Collaborative Learning in Adult Education', in *ERIC Digest*, No 113, 1991 (retrieved from ERIC database). (ED334469).

6   Bronwen Cowie and Beverley Bell, 'A Model of Formative Assessment in Science Education', in *Assessment in Education: Principles, Policy and Practice*, Vol 6, No 1, 1 March 1999.

CHAPTER 19

COMPETITIONS AND GENDERS: A FEMINIST APPROACH

Discussion with the Hi-VIS Feminist Design Collective

Question (Q): It seems that most of the Hi-VIS participants have a direct experience of architecture competitions, either as students or working in an office environment. How would you describe this experience, and did you notice any gender issues/concerns at any stage in the process, ie preparation, submission or a competition's aftermath?

We have generally taken working as students on competitions as a learning experience, and so our criticality of the process and the politics of competitions, as well as our understanding of the labour and time used, hasn't been acute. However, in the professional environment, a few things have become apparent.

First, it has been quite evident for us that the short bursts of long hours that form the competition scenario

of work inherently assumes that participants don't have other priorities, ie they are able to drop the life they have outside of work for that period because it is not a life in which they are depended on, such as for care and domestic or emotional labour, also known as Reproductive Labour or Social Reproduction (to be elaborated upon later in the discussion).

In our experience, this 'dropping' of priorities has not only been praised but has also become an expectation, meaning that those who cannot do this for whatever reason are looked down upon. If women are a new emergence in contemporary forms of work (though a re-emergence into labour outside the home, as the 'domestic' structure forming in parallel with early capitalist development in the 16th century), then it goes without saying that as these periods of labour intensity, which are also the main opportunities to perform or excel in front of bosses, etc, this is exclusionary for those who have other (mainly unpaid) labours to consider, predominantly women. The ability to win should be based on [women's] talent rather than their potential to disregard other commitments – the fact they are praised for this highlights a huge workplace lacuna.

We should also highlight issues around the economic stability required to commit to the work hours required during competition time when children or other dependencies are involved. If childcare can be paid for until 2am, for example, then mothers are able to commit; if this is not the case, they experience further exclusion for not prioritising work. Who pays for this if it's not through inter-generational privilege or marital support? Does it come for free along with the takeaway pizza delivery to the office at 8pm?

We're not saying we want this all-nighter life to be equal for all, however, the slog of the competition period in terms of work hours is an unhealthy practice that we want to abolish for everyone. We just feel that this aspect is especially problematic because it reproduces gender hierarchies in the workplace with regard to commitment, making those with 'other' undervalued

and invisible commitments appear less committed [to workplace commitments]. We don't deny the feeling of accomplishment gained upon achieving a submission, either; but we *would* sacrifice this for generally better working conditions that enable us to remove the 'suffering = working' mentality prevalent in architecture today.

Q: Architecture competitions, especially when open and anonymous, are related to democratic processes: everyone has the chance to enter and win on the basis of their abilities and talent. Do you think this is still the case today, with the proliferation of competitions by invitation? Have you noticed any gender-related issues around the processes of 'closed' competitions for the client, organiser and invited participants?

The idea that competitions might be open in some equal or universally accessible manner is a farce, in that access to resources – from printers to interns to parents paying rent while you set yourself up – vary between participants, and cannot be known by the blanket call-out of 'open competitions'. With competition by invitation, we have witnessed female-run practices that pretty much mothered a way of design then were sidelined on an invitation list for younger, male-dominated practices which had worked for, learned from, and taken contacts from them in the first place. This might seem like standard practice on the part of the younger opportunist keen to make an early splash in the profession, and it is. What makes it gendered is that established male-run practices tend to be more of a 'name' to have on the invitation list than their female counterparts, and younger male-run practices are cushioned by the confidence that comes from the proliferation of male success in the profession. This results in issues at both ends of the scale: men appear to have learned the 'soft touch', but have the natural ability to 'get the job done', with no 'flouncing' or whatever (there might indeed be flouncing from a predominantly male environment having to deal with a substantial presence of women around ...), whereas women lose the right of practising which they fought hard to establish.

Of course, we should face the Zaha Hadid (the famous female architect) retort now. We could say a number of things about this, but will settle with mentioning how exclusion is furthered by tokenism as the exception that proves the rule (ie that it's *even noticeable* says enough). In the end, tokenism often allows unjust structures and their proponents to deflect criticism with their singular piece of evidence of 'diversity'. We could say the same for David Adjaye (the famous black architect). It is not enough to have a droplet of 'other' in a sea of the same.

Q: Would you rather work on open calls (usually calls for ideas) initiated by various organisations?

We, along with others, dream of the Greater London Council (GLC) and the time when it wasn't only private capital that steered the direction of architecture, but an institutionally social agenda and structure. These days are gone for now, and marginalising socially conscious/ ethical work within the NGO/charity sector is in itself a tragedy; another enclave that enables poor practice to continue. There are infinite ways this could be better, but it's as long as a piece of string.

Something else we experienced is that it is not necessarily those with the talent and abilities who present projects at interview, but those who support the demographic of the client or organisation. This can often ensure that a male counterpart is included in the interview process, regardless of his input to the competition, simply in order to represent and connect to the panel, who (surprise surprise) are more likely to be male. Interestingly, however, a *small* female presence on judging panels is often appreciated, which in many ways relates to the idea of women as 'support' for the work of men – able to see the broader and more nuanced effects of a project produced in a short amount of time, but not necessarily the protagonists of ideas themselves.

Q: Competitions create 'exhaustion' in the effort to comply with submission deadlines. Do you think structuring the competition time differently can support processes of 'experimentation' by giving time to develop ideas and enjoy the unfolding of invention as you go along? Current processes of 'acceleration' are approached either by applying even more intense accelerationisms (to speed up the process to its limit) or by slowing processes down to disrupt systems and structures. As a feminist design collective, would you be interested to approach the 'time of competition' differently?

One aspect that we've noticed persists even in conditions where gender is not addressed directly is that people who were raised as women have a tendency to have been taught to pick up the slack, often in a way that is directly related to the actions and operations men engage in. We have noticed this in work environments, both in terms of the production of architecture itself, and in terms of the supportive work – cleaning the empty coffee cups, etc. Women unquestioningly and undeclaratively pick up these support tasks significantly more often than men. Within the structures of time limits, these roles are magnified tenfold, and women tend to keep things ticking along from the periphery as the spontaneity of good ideas can be produced in the comfort of this support.

A feminist analysis has established that accelerationism stems from a privileged (often male) Left rather than an oppressed, 'nothing-to-lose' demographic, and does not take into account the real lives already at the brink of collapse that would suffer even further under strategies that celebrate and push for more instability. That said, there is naivety in simply 'slowing down' as a means of resistance to this; resistance comes in the 'blocking' of capital flows and the 'breaking through' of state boundaries – active confrontation rather than a tentative clinging as prevention.

Acceleration of time can cause deceleration of pure production, making us lapse into establishing verifiable protocol to allow for 'success' rather than more progressive design that might challenge the structural injustices we find in our profession at a wider scale through our work. It forces everyone into a fast consumption of ideas and outputs; some considered, some natural, some forced by the process. The role of women in a positive sense, natural or not, tends toward a multi-faceted approach that considers numerous layers of production and impact – let's call it the child of 'can do two things at once'. This means that the design-time pressure of a competition often does not allow for this particular design quality, especially if projects are to be critical of the status quo or

[are] following 'feeling' that is worked out rather than 'conditioning' that is formulaic.

Q: Would you consider alternative ways to experiment outside competitions, or would you choose to move beyond the scientific tradition of experimentation, to which competitions belong, establishing verifiable protocols to secure process and outcomes?

With relation to the architectural competition, we would be interested in a 'limited time' that corresponds with a 'particular location' for the entry to be produced, and thus a limited number of bodies, resources and drawings that can be used. It's not just about a regulation of the quantity of work, but about highlighting the valuable remnants of a competition scenario. What would it mean to bring the unknown other into a room with the 'big star', physically working under the same conditions and with the same possibilities and constraints? It would, ethics aside, allow for a more rigorous scientific approach with verifiable protocols, secure processes and thus 'more reliable' outcomes. While we might be fetishising process (and avoiding the thought of the administration), it is because the process as it stands is what is most problematic and unjust. A re-imagining of this could create not only a 'fair' space of

production but also the work itself would then respond to the brief, the site, and the conditions in a way that is sincere. What we mean is that further critique could emerge of the content of each and every competition if the process through which entrants participate were equal. This would probably need to go hand in hand with anonymisation of entry or pseudonym authors. As a group, we are also interested in modes of authorship from a feminist perspective. We see that all work is collectively produced, and that it is often masculine structures that have produced the need to be named, and thus, rather than submitting to the tag of the 'anonymous' and allowing macho ego brandings to persist, we sign our work as a collective person.

Q: Competitions, and especially the category of ideas competitions, have been linked with the condition in which architects freed from restrictions can 'experiment' and develop their inventive abilities. This is usually experienced as a refreshing break from professional work on commissions.

In theory, there is a wonderful scenario produced by the competition that can free architects from 'reality' as such, both intellectually and practically. Competitions can be used to test out an idea, platform an agenda, critique current practice and imagine a future, be that utopic or dystopic, feasible or absurd. There have been competitions and entries that, even if they didn't win or couldn't be built, have caused seismic shifts in architectural discourse and paved the way for a new way of thinking; we are thinking of the *Haus am Horn* by George Muche, Archizoom's No-stop City, and Venturi Scott Brown's Academia Bridge (whose architects are arguably the most famous example of gender discrimination and female-sidelining). We might argue that the fact that there isn't this freedom or support for alternative thinking outside of exploitative labour conditions isn't so cool anyway, however. Nevertheless, the heterotopic nature of the competition, which enables a reality to be seen through the reflection caused by a hypothetical 'mirror',[1] is something that should be held onto dearly, as one of the last corners of architectural agency that isn't subsumed into capitalist processes. For women, LGBTQ and BAME groups, this moment can be seminal: with 'nothing to lose' intellectually or creatively, and if the aforementioned responsibilities and restrictions on the boundaries between work and life are put aside for a second, the competition is a crack in reality from which radical gestures and critique can emerge.

Q: How do you feel about the competition as an 'exemplary moment' of architectural practice, and about aggressively competitive structures as a whole?

We should begin by saying that we will be specific to the competition, though there is of course so much to say with regard to the architectural practice in general. We will stick to the topic of how this inherently masculine structure of material and immaterial labour feeds directly into the scenarios of the competition which, because it is seen as an epitome of architectural practice, thus symbiotically reproduces these structures back out again into the day-to-day.

In relation to the general concept of competition as such, we would say that during the design phase of competitions, male behaviours (fostered from an early age) – ie the willingness to present ideas without invitation, disregard of professional hierarchies, speaking up, etc – puts them in the centre of the competition design process. On the other hand, the behaviour encouraged in women – waiting until asked to speak, listening to others without interrupting, etc – means that female assistants are frequently resigned to the periphery, merely supporting the execution of the design team's ideas that have been forefronted by men. This manifests the idea of Reproductive Labour, one of the most significant developments of Marxism in the 21st century, that places women at the foundation of modern-day capitalism precisely through their enslavement as 'support' for male workers: 'the sexual division of labour was above all a power relation, a division within the work-force, while being an immense boost to capital accumulation'.[2]

It is said that creativity flourishes when value is given to the output before it has been made. The energy of the architect can then be put into the design process rather than bound up in a concern for winning.

The Reproductive Labour mentioned throughout this interview, no matter how crucial, goes unnoticed as part of this process; this is its essence. This means that so much of a 'woman's work' is not given a distinguishable, quantifiable value, while it stretches infinitely into all those nuanced levels of support and nurturing that produce more fertile ground for better design.

All in all, competitions are like a replication of this pattern of controlling, reward-driven process under the guise of a moment for brilliance. Combine that with general bourgeois notions of 'equality' that the open competition apparently champions, and you cement the meritocracy that stands in contrast to so many factors that render that perfect lab condition an untrue reflection of our social reality.

Q: As a feminist design collective, would you ever be interested in organising an architecture competition, and why? If yes, what competitions' structures, forms and content would you like to design differently?

We're so busy trying to produce spaces or moments of truly collective work, and that requires so much labour in a world so hell-bent against it, that sure, why not? It would be great to challenge the small but deeply rooted and heavily disempowering cruxes of the competition structure. The competition would then challenge its own status as 'exemplary'. If there could be a better micro-politics, between individuals or in limited periods of time, it would no doubt influence the possibility of a better situation in the broader context. Theatre is practice for revolution.

Notes

1. Michel foucault, *The Order of Things: An Archaeology of the Human Sciences* (London: Routledge Classics, 2001).

2. Silvia Federici, *Caliban and the Witch: Women, the Body, and Primitive Accumulation* (Brooklyn NY: Autonomedia, 2004).

AFTERWORD

Antigoni Katsakou and Maria Theodorou

More than 30 authors of 15 different nationalities, disciplines, and social and professional contexts have contributed to the making of this book. If nothing else, this broad participation illustrates the subject's range of interest and diversity; its interdisciplinary and complex nature. After all, competitions are inseparably linked to the production of the built environment as a social matter that affects almost everyone's lives and well-being.

Competitions are without doubt a controversial topic: they have been (and will continue to be) discussed both as architectural 'creativity feasts', and 'blood-sucking beasts' of the profession; as instigators of innovation, and obsolete mechanisms for the misuse of a profuse cultural and financial capital; as grounds for discussion and consensus, and biased spaces of eclectic favouritism; as waste fields of inspiration and hope, and idealised, artistic challenges for excellence. However, through the illustration of different cases, it has been possible to establish that experimentation is possible within the competitions' background and processual framework; experimentation in the sense of testing new ideas which may refer to all of competitions' varied facets and intricate structure, and therefore be understood in terms of procedures, architectural design and its representational vocabulary, social and political settings.

Competitions seem to have entered a new era, in which advanced technology and computer-aided performance have become primordial parameters of the game, calling for its rules to be revisited and redefined. This seems to be particularly true regarding two potential axes of experimentation: the visibility of information referring to competitive procedures and procurement frameworks, and the assessment of architectural quality through submissions' comparable qualities. Electronic information databases, free and easy to access, as well as computer software facilitating the evaluation of commensurable features of projects, are some of the research avenues marking the future of competitions.

As far as competition procedures go, exchange of experiences on the international level is of crucial importance. It was among the editors' intentions to open up the debate around competitions by gathering together accounts from various geographical contexts. Countries with a rich competition tradition, especially a long-lasting, regulated one, can offer alternative models of competition organising: in these, dialogue among the involved parties is promoted at an early stage of the design process, even in the brief-writing phase. Thus, building projects take up their final form and become implemented on a basis of broad unanimity. Experimentation in these cases refers to adaptations of conventional competition types and possibly incremental innovations that can bring about positive change.

The future of competitions will also essentially be built through testing based on reconsideration of the past. As far as the social and political background goes, the involvement and consultation of various social layers into a building project, and into a potentially competition-born one, although typical of the last quarter of the 20th century, can still produce valid results in the present day through the enhancing of the private initiative, and through collective efforts emerging at the bottom of the social pyramid. The architectural design needs solid foundations that must be laid onto the real problems of its social and political context, and to efficient descriptions of the problems at hand. In bonding with the social and political context, the role of the architects' representatives and their professional organisations seems crucial.

Competitions represent for architects a way of securing commissions and work. Through the discussions in this book, it has been demonstrated that they may also be crucial, if not for the survival of an architectural firm, but certainly for its development, either in the form of an initial career boost or in the form of a walking crutch in periods of recess. Thus, it is sometimes difficult to discern whether architects' ambition is motivated by necessity or driven by a collective professional conscience and a belief in the profession's artistic attributes. Inconsistencies do appear, but such paradoxes also help to interrogate current practices and established strategies, and encourage adopting better ones.

Another intention of the editors of this book was to provide sufficient room for the architect's voice, both the theorist and practitioner, to be heard. Strange as it may seem, this is not often the case in matters that directly affect the architects' practice: research space is frequently taken over by other disciplines. Although architects may in this case provide the 'inside' view of the things and therefore are less objective, their first-hand accounts of the possibilities offered, as well as of the recurring problems created by competitions, should surely serve as starting points for interrogation.

Architects are supposedly the ones best equipped to tackle architectural design, and this is what competitions are all about; in this sense, experimentation refers to a quest for a superior quality of architectural work, generated by an inherent connection with its contemporary social context.

Most professionals seem to agree that competitions can offer grounds for testing new concepts. But what are the qualities that this 'newness' implies, in terms of its authors, the cultural models it addresses and the living ways it attempts to promote? Is experimentation, and even more so innovation, a privilege of the young? Or for that matter, is it a privilege of disinterested creativity and sacrifice, which seem to be taken for granted as far as architectural practice in the background of competitions is concerned, both by the lay public and the architects? Is the production of architectural design and the built environment a matter of frustrated individuals that can hardly find their place in the social arena, overpowered by developers, civil engineers, contractors or politicians? Is the desired result a 'competition' architecture that answers to ephemeral ideals and impressions devoid of essence, destined to deceive and soon become outdated?

The role of professional organisations seems all-important: in the education of clients, of young architects, and the public. Apart from defending their members' rights, and securing alternatives for a correct and manageable workload, professional bodies need to take on board the social parameters of the design; to walk hand in hand with the demands of a global society, and its mixed local and international profile. Competitions need to be brought forward in public life; a point has to be made of the fact that they are often the starting point of important 'stills' of cultural achievements, and of successful regeneration practices of the city.

Competitions constitute a fairly young field of research; as spaces of social, professional, political and financial interaction, they need to be further examined and analysed systematically.

This book offers an impression of the current situation, and attempts to identify potential avenues for the future development of the competition institution; the objective being to discern the questions that need to be asked, and advance in assessing likely solutions.

INDEX

PICTURE CREDITS